Sandwich Bay

D1271651

THE OPEN
CHAMPIONSHIP
1993

THE OPEN CHAMPIONSHIP 1993

WRITERS

ROBERT SOMMERS
RAYMOND JACOBS
MICHAEL MCDONNELL
MICHAEL WILLIAMS
MARINO PARASCENZO
ALISTER NICOL
JOHN HOPKINS

PHOTOGRAPHERS

LAWRENCE LEVY
MICHAEL COHEN

EDITOR

BEV NORWOOD

AUTHORISED BY THE
CHAMPIONSHIP COMMITTEE
OF THE ROYAL AND ANCIENT
GOLF CLUB OF ST ANDREWS

TRANSWORLD PUBLISHERS LTD
61-63 Uxbridge Road, London W5 5SA

TRANSWORLD PUBLISHERS (AUSTRALIA) PTY LTD
15-23 Helles Avenue, Moorebank, NSW 2170

TRANSWORLD PUBLISHERS (NZ) LTD
Cnr Moselle and Waipareira Aves,
Henderson, Auckland

Published 1993 by Partridge Press
a division of Transworld Publishers Ltd
Copyright © 1993 The Championship Committee Merchandising
Limited

Statistics of 122nd Open Championship produced on a
Unisys Computer System

Photographs on pp. 14-15, 53, 69 courtesy of Danielle Fluer
Photographs on pp. 18-21 courtesy of Brian Morgan

A CIP catalogue record for this book is available
from the British Library

185225 2081

Typeset by Davis Design
Printed in Great Britain
by Bath Press Colourbooks, Glasgow

CONTENTS

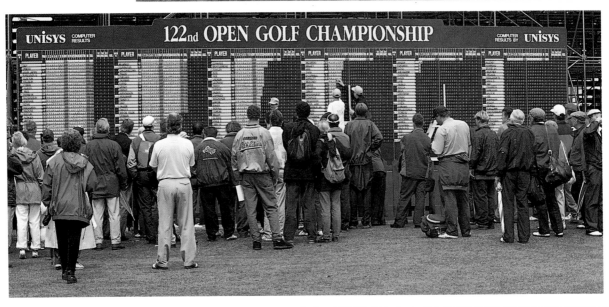

INTRODUCTION

BY R. H. EVANS, C. B. E.
Chief Executive
British Aerospace plc

After last year's dramatic final-hole triumph by Nick Faldo at Muirfield, even more excitement was in store at Royal St George's Golf Club as Greg Norman set a championship record while winning by two strokes over Faldo and by three over Bernhard Langer, with most of the world's best golfers in close pursuit.

British Aerospace were once again very proud to be involved in this great sporting occasion. Over the years, our friends and business colleagues from around the world have enjoyed the unique atmosphere of the Open Championship. We look forward to welcoming them in 1994 to Turnberry, the scene of Norman's first Open Championship victory in 1986 and the epic duel between Tom Watson and Jack Nicklaus in 1977.

R. H. Evans, C. B. E.

THE CHAMPIONSHIP COMMITTEE

CHAIRMAN

W. G. N. ROACH

DEPUTY CHAIRMAN

A. R. COLE-HAMILTON

COMMITTEE

M. VANS AGNEW
J. E. COOK
R. M. E. DAVITT
M. C. GRINT
D. J. HARRISON
R. H. PALMER
P. M. G. UNSWORTH
W. J. UZIELLI
R. P. WHITE
R. S. WHITMORE

BUSINESS SUB-COMMITTEE CHAIRMAN

H. M. CAMPBELL

RULES SUB-COMMITTEE CHAIRMAN

J. L. S. PASQUILL

ADDITIONAL MEMBER

G. B. OVENS
COUNCIL OF NATIONAL GOLF UNIONS

SECRETARY

M. F. BONALLACK, OBE

DEPUTY SECRETARY

W. G. WILSON

CHAMPIONSHIP SECRETARY

D. HILL

ASSISTANT SECRETARY (CHAMPIONSHIPS)

D. R. WEIR

INTRODUCTION

BY W. G. N. ROACH
Chairman of Championship Committee
Royal and Ancient Golf Club of St Andrews

The 122nd Open Championship will be remembered as one of the most memorable — many of the greatest players in the world locked together for the final 36 holes with some fantastic scoring until at the very end a worthy and popular winner emerged. Let us not forget those who came so close to winning only to fail on the final few holes.

Before the championship began there was serious concern at the very dry conditions which had prevailed for several weeks. The course was very hard and perhaps unfair. The eve of the championship brought heavy rain which made conditions near perfect.

The Championship Committee are grateful to the Royal St George's Golf Club for the courtesy of their course. We would also like to thank the many hundreds of volunteers for their help during the week.

Royal St George's has a distinguished history, although not always considered an ideal championship venue. No doubt Dr Laidlaw Purves, the founder, would have been astonished at the treatment given to the course with scores in the low 60s. He would certainly have been proud had he heard the praise given by the great players competing for the world's oldest title.

The week was completed with the appearance of Gene Sarazen who, in a charming little speech, talked of the awesome skill he had witnessed. The greatest he had ever seen.

We again acknowledge and appreciate the support of British Aerospace in the publication of this official annual record, and we thank the photographers and writers for their efforts in producing this worthy memento of the championship.

W. G. N. Roach

FOREWORD

BY GREG NORMAN

To think that I started at Royal St George's with a 6, a double bogey on the first hole, it goes to show that you should never get too discouraged when something doesn't go as you planned. I have always been a believer in being positive, in life and on the golf course, and I have always believed in my ability to do anything I wanted to do.

My thanks go to my wife, Laura, who has shared the bad times and the good; to my coach, Butch Harmon, and to many friends and supporters who have always been behind me.

That final round was one you just dream about. I cannot say in my whole career that I have played a round and not missed one shot, but that day I never mis-hit a shot. I hit every drive perfectly, every iron perfectly, and only made a mess of one putt, that very short putt on the 17th.

I was enjoying the championship so much, I wished it wouldn't finish.

I knew I had to play well because of the calibre of golfers around me — Bernhard Langer, Nick Faldo, Corey Pavin, Nick Price, Peter Senior, Fred Couples and the rest, people whom we all regard as the best players in the game. I loved that competition.

We knew from the first round onwards that this would be one of the best Open Championships ever, and the best that anyone could ever win. I was never thinking of setting records, only of staying focused and wanting to win, and this was the best I ever played in my life. To win this championship, the most important golf title in the world, and to win against those players, means everything.

Greg Norman

11

122ND OPEN CHAMPIONSHIP

*Denotes amateurs

NAME	SCORES				TOTAL	MONEY
Greg Norman, Australia	66	68	69	64	267	£100,000
Nick Faldo, England	69	63	70	67	269	80,000
Bernhard Langer, Germany	67	66	70	67	270	67,000
Peter Senior, Australia	66	69	70	67	272	50,500
Corey Pavin, USA	68	66	68	70	272	50,500
Paul Lawrie, Scotland	72	68	69	65	274	33,167
Ernie Els, South Africa	68	69	69	68	274	33,167
Nick Price, Zimbabwe	68	70	67	69	274	33,167
Scott Simpson, USA	68	70	71	66	275	25,500
Fred Couples, USA	68	66	72	69	275	25,500
Wayne Grady, Australia	74	68	64	69	275	25,500
Payne Stewart, USA	71	72	70	63	276	21,500
Barry Lane, England	70	68	71	68	277	20,500
Mark Calcavecchia, USA	66	73	71	68	278	15,214
Tom Kite, USA	72	70	68	68	278	15,214
Mark McNulty, Zimbabwe	67	71	71	69	278	15,214
Gil Morgan, USA	70	68	70	70	278	15,214
Jose Rivero, Spain	68	73	67	70	278	15,214
Fuzzy Zoeller, USA	66	70	71	71	278	15,214
John Daly, USA	71	66	70	71	278	15,214
Peter Baker, England	70	67	74	68	279	10,000
Jesper Parnevik, Sweden	68	74	68	69	279	10,000
Howard Clark, England	67	72	70	70	279	10,000
Mark Roe, England	70	71	73	66	280	8,400
David Frost, South Africa	69	73	70	68	280	8,400
Rodger Davis, Australia	68	71	71	70	280	8,400
Malcolm Mackenzie, England	72	71	71	67	281	7,225
Yoshinori Mizumaki, Japan	69	69	73	70	281	7,225
Des Smyth, Ireland	67	74	70	70	281	7,225
Larry Mize, USA	67	69	74	71	281	7,225
Mark James, England	70	70	70	71	281	7,225
* Iain Pyman, England	68	72	70	71	281	Medal
Seve Ballesteros, Spain	68	73	69	71	281	7,225
Jean Van De Velde, France	75	67	73	67	282	6,180
Paul Broadhurst, England	71	69	74	68	282	6,180
Wayne Westner, South Africa	67	73	72	70	282	6,180
Raymond Floyd, USA	70	72	67	73	282	6,180
Howard Twitty, USA	71	71	67	73	282	6,180
Rocco Mediate, USA	71	71	72	69	283	5,328
Carl Mason, England	69	73	72	69	283	5,328
Andrew Magee, USA	71	72	71	69	283	5,328
Greg Turner, New Zealand	67	76	70	70	283	5,328
Duffy Waldorf, USA	68	71	73	71	283	5,328
Paul Moloney, Australia	70	71	71	71	283	5,328
Anders Sorensen, Denmark	69	70	72	72	283	5,328
Christy O'Connor, Jr., Ireland	72	68	69	74	283	5,328
Darren Clarke, N. Ireland	69	71	69	74	283	5,328
John Huston, USA	68	73	76	67	284	4,850

Steve Elkington, Australia	72	71	71	70	284	4,850
Lee Janzen, USA	69	71	73	71	284	4,850
Ian Garbutt, England	68	75	73	69	285	4,356
Stephen Ames, Trinadad and Tobago	67	75	73	70	285	4,356
Miguel Angel Jimenez, Spain	69	74	72	70	285	4,356
Ian Woosnam, Wales	72	71	72	70	285	4,356
Sam Torrance, Scotland	72	70	72	71	285	4,356
Frank Nobilo, New Zealand	69	70	74	72	285	4,356
Manuel Pinero, Spain	70	72	71	72	285	4,356
Jonathan Sewell, England	70	72	69	74	285	4,356
Paul Azinger, USA	69	73	74	70	286	4,025
Tom Lehman, USA	69	71	73	73	286	4,025
Vijay Singh, Fiji	69	72	72	73	286	4,025
Craig Parry, Australia	72	69	71	74	286	4,025
Ross Drummond, Scotland	73	67	76	71	287	3,850
Olle Karlsson, Sweden	70	71	73	73	287	3,850
James Spence, England	69	72	72	74	287	3,850
James Cook, England	71	71	74	72	288	3,675
Magnus Sunesson, Sweden	70	73	73	72	288	3,675
William Guy, Scotland	70	73	73	72	288	3,675
Tom Pernice, USA	73	70	70	75	288	3,675
Mike Miller, England	73	68	76	72	289	3,517
Tom Purtzer, USA	70	70	74	75	289	3,517
Ian Baker-Finch, Australia	73	69	67	80	289	3,517
Dan Forsman, USA	71	70	76	73	290	3,500
Peter Fowler, Australia	74	69	74	73	290	3,500
Peter Mitchell, England	73	70	72	75	290	3,500
Mike Harwood, Australia	72	70	72	76	290	3,500
Mikael Krantz, Sweden	77	66	72	77	292	3,500
Ricky Willison, England	73	70	74	76	293	3,500

NON QUALIFIERS AFTER 36 HOLES
(All professionals receive £600)

Eoghan O'Connell, Ireland	74 70	144
Tony Johnstone, Zimbabwe	72 72	144
Costantino Rocca, Italy	71 73	144
Chip Beck, USA	73 71	144
Jack Nicklaus, USA	69 75	144
Robert Allenby, Australia	69 75	144
Donnie Hammond, USA	69 75	144
Glen Day, USA	67 77	144
Gary Player, South Africa	73 71	144
Billy Andrade, USA	70 74	144
Tom Watson, USA	71 73	144
Davis Love III, USA	70 74	144
Fulton Allem, South Africa	73 71	144
David Edwards, USA	76 68	144
Colin Montgomerie, Scotland	74 70	144
Philip Talbot, England	70 74	144
Katsuyoshi Tomori, Japan	71 73	144
Martin Gates, England	72 73	145
John Cook, USA	73 72	145
Vicente Fernandez, Argentina	73 72	145
Jeff Maggert, USA	72 73	145
Anders Forsbrand, Sweden	71 74	145
Ben Crenshaw, USA	70 75	145
Edwardo Romero, Argentina	73 72	145
Retief Goosen, South Africa	69 76	145
Steven Richardson, England	72 73	145
Lanny Wadkins, USA	72 73	145
Paul McGinley, Ireland	73 72	145
Gary Evans, England	67 78	145
Craig Cassells, England	68 77	145
Bill Malley, USA	74 71	145
De Wet Basson, South Africa	72 74	146
Jeff Sluman, USA	74 72	146
Robert Karlsson, Sweden	74 72	146
Paul Way, England	72 74	146
Mats Hallberg, Sweden	69 77	146
Robert Lee, England	72 74	146
Sandy Lyle, Scotland	70 76	146
Richard Boxall, England	71 75	146
Jim Gallagher, Jr., USA	73 74	147
Chen Tze Ming, Taiwan	73 74	147
Mark O'Meara, USA	71 76	147
Jose Maria Olazabal, Spain	73 74	147
Naomichi Ozaki, Japan	70 77	147
Joakim Haeggman, Sweden	73 74	147
David Gilford, England	72 75	147
Jim McGovern, USA	74 74	148
* Michael Welch, England	74 74	148
Takaaki Fukuzawa, Japan	73 75	148
Per-Ulrik Johansson, Sweden	69 79	148
Steve Pate, USA	79 69	148
* Justin Leonard, USA	74 74	148
Stephen Field, England	72 76	148
Brad Faxon, USA	70 79	149
Roger Chapman, England	73 76	149
Gordon Brand, Jr., Scotland	70 79	149
Mark Davis, England	74 75	149
Peter Smith, Scotland	75 74	149
Michael Clayton, Australia	72 77	149
David Feherty, N. Ireland	77 72	149
Tony Jacklin, England	73 76	149
Jose Carriles, Spain	76 73	149
Brian Watts, USA	72 77	149
Benoit Telleria, France	73 77	150
Terry Price, Australia	72 78	150
Gary Orr, Scotland	72 78	150
Andrew Sherborne, England	73 78	151
Tony Nash, England	70 81	151
Larry Rinker, USA	78 73	151
Paul Eales, England	73 78	151
Graham Farr, England	73 79	152
Peter Scott, England	73 79	152
* Stephen Dundas, Scotland	76 77	153
Ryoken Kawagishi, Japan	79 76	155
* Mitch Voges, USA	80 75	155
Noboru Sugai, Japan	74 82	156
* Simon Griffiths, England	77 81	158
Nico Van Rensburg, S. Afr.	82 77	159

Scenes from Sandwich, including St Clements Church (above left), from where Dr Laidlaw Purves 'spied the land with a

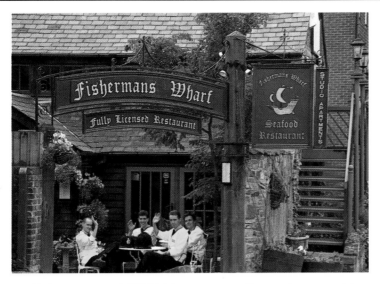

golfer's eye' (previous page, bottom).

ROUND ROYAL ST GEORGE'S

No. 1 441 Yards, Par 4

The introduction is in complete character with what follows — demanding. The right side of the 'Kitchen,' as the valley across the fairway has been called for almost a century, is the preferred driving area. That achieved, the second shot over the guarding bunkers becomes more straightforward, but if the encouragement of an instant birdie is to be achieved, the ball has to be quickly brought to a halt.

No. 2 376 Yards, Par 4

A hole more susceptible to a birdie. The carry over the dominant bunker is not formidable, but the fairway is a quiltwork of humps and hollows almost certain to leave an awkward stance. The safer tee shot is to the right, but that leaves the player with a more testing approach.

No. 3 210 Yards, Par 3

Regarded now as being the most exacting of the four short holes. A long iron or more is needed to a narrow shelf of green — visible now, whereas until the mid-1970s the tee shot was blind to a punchbowl green. There are no bunkers, but rough and banks lie in wait for the wayward ball.

No. 4 468 Yards, Par 4

The yawning bunker gouged into the face of a towering dune makes this drive among the most confrontational in championship golf. It can be carried, but unless to the right of the fairway the golfer cannot see the green tucked into a hillside.

No. 5 421 Yards, Par 4

The key to mastering this left-hand dogleg is to drive to a place not only of safety but which grants a sight of the flagstick between the dunes, beyond which there is a good deal of dead ground — and a first glimpse of the sea and the cliffs of Ramsgate on the far shore.

No. 6 155 Yards, Par 3

The 'Maiden,' the high dune on the left of the green (which in Ian Fleming's James Bond novel, *Goldfinger*, became the 'Virgin') is the dominant feature. However, the greater problem lies in judging the breeze. The tee shot is to a target which, although down in a bowl, is assiduously defended by four bunkers.

No. 7 530 Yards, Par 5

The course's first par 5 but not, particularly in a northeast wind, to be regarded as an easy mark for a birdie. The drive must carry some 200 yards over a well-bunkered ridge to the concealed expanse of a fairway which dips down and angles to the left, following the adjacent shoreline.

No. 8 418 Yards, Par 4

This hole, once a par 3, is an appealing challenge, although never an easy one playing into the prevailing wind. The drive aims to reach a plateau, after which the fairway gradually descends to a long and undulating green, especially difficult to hold from the right rough. Short of the target is a broad belt of rough and scrub.

No. 9 389 Yards, Par 4

A hole which frequently proves to be more of a test than its modest measurement might suggest. The problems facing the golfer are twofold — to shape the drive through a valley to hold the fairway, favouring the right side so as to make the green, typical of these links for its angle and large contours, more accessible for the second shot.

No. 10 399 Yards, Par 4

Where Tom Kite's meteor fell to earth eight years ago. Leading the championship by two strokes, he pulled his approach to the elevated, exposed target into the first left-hand bunker, proceeded from there into the second, thinned his fourth over the green, and never recovered from a double-bogey 6.

No. 11 216 Yards, Par 3

The substitute short hole for the original eighth, with a restructured green from the time when this was a short par 4. It is well bunkered and although the tee shot, even for professionals, can call for the driver, the holing-out putts are its feature. No member of the host club, it is said, ever concedes a putt here.

No. 12 365 Yards, Par 4

The refreshment hut beside this green has helped to restore many a weary pilgrim. The competitors will think of the hole more as another birdie offering, provided they safely make the carry over the bunkered ridge and then negotiate a quite straightforward second shot.

No. 13 443 Yards, Par 4

The start of the sting in the course's tail, more identifiable with the Dragon than St George. An angled drive over a long ridge of wild country and the ball still cannot be seen to be on the fairway or not. The second shot is aimed at the clubhouse at Prince's (where Gene Sarazen won in 1932) to a long green, bunkered on both sides and with out-of-bounds behind.

No. 14 507 Yards, Par 5

The only hole on the course with a flat fairway and an out-of-bounds fence to menace the drive on the right. There is little leeway on the left either, but a good tee shot should eliminate the stream across the fairway, the Suez Canal, as a serious hazard and make the green a genuine target.

No. 15 466 Yards, Par 4

One of the finest two-shot holes in championship golf. The drive must be threaded between bunkers on either side of the fairway, but a more severe challenge still lies in the second shot. It has to carry cross bunkers to an oddly shaped green.

No. 16 163 Yards, Par 3

Where Tony Jacklin had British television's first live hole-in-one in the 1967 Dunlop Masters. Isolated amid the bunkers and mounds, the large green is not as constricted as it looks. Play safe and a long first putt becomes probable, be bold and the likelihood is that access to the hole is threatened by one of those deep hazards.

No. 17 425 Yards, Par 4

Position from the tee is again of great importance on another fairway far from being a level playing field, but again the greater test comes with the second shot. The raised green is much wider than it is deep and in front of it is a hollow which frequently confuses judgement of clubbing.

No. 18 468 Yards, Par 4

No let up on an exacting last hole, where the drive should ideally hold to the left side of the fairway to take out of play the bunker which encroaches on the right of the green. On the left is the hollow where, in 1922, George Duncan failed to get down in two to tie with Walter Hagen. Sixty-three years later Sandy Lyle did likewise, but in his case 5 still gave him victory.

VICTORIES AGAINST THE GRAIN

BY RAYMOND JACOBS

Royal St George's has, with perhaps the notable exception of two players, produced winners of the Open Championship whose victories went against the grain both of precedent and of expectation. Harry Vardon, who won the title over the Kent links for the third time in 1899 and for the fifth time 12 years later, and Walter Hagen, who returned to win his third Open here in 1928, six years after having done so for the first time, failed to conform to the pattern established before and since by the eight others. The maverick character of the examination they passed has been reflected in the quirky circumstances of their victories.

In 1894, when the championship was first held at St George's, a mere seven years after its opening, J.H. Taylor became the first English professional to win. Jack White, 10 years on, was the first winner whose total was less than 300 (by four strokes, in fact) and the three other championships played between the two world wars also had very distinctive outcomes. In 1922 Hagen was the first American-born winner; in 1934 Henry Cotton brought an end to an unbroken sequence

Dr Laidlaw Purves

of 10 United States' successes; and in 1938 Reg Whitcombe steadfastly defied appalling conditions on the final day for his victory, the last to be gained at Sandwich until four years after hostilities had ceased.

Bobby Locke then had the first of his four victories, by 12 strokes after a 36-hole play-off with Harry Bradshaw. There was then an interval of 32 years before the Open returned to the course. It is by no means overstating the case to say that had it not been decided in the late 1970s to build a ring road around the ancient town — historic in its own picturesque right as a Royal Cinque Port but also notorious as a bottleneck to traffic — the Royal and Ancient Golf Club never would have restored Royal St George's to the championship roster. The links would have been left in their southern solitude to history, to the larks' song and, not least, to the members.

When the R and A learned that this asphalt equivalent of a heart-bypass operation was to be performed by the local authority, which itself saw how important a relief road would become to the area, reality changed thinking. Some of the town's tradespeople thought they would lose business in normal times, but as one resident remarked: 'You can't park in Sandwich anyway and the effect has been to make it a nicer place.' Pessimistic forecasts of traffic congestion reduced the predicted attendance in 1981, but although there were problems on the first two days in 1985 the flow subsequently improved, despite some 30,000 more spectators having to be channelled in and out.

Since the R and A had never completely given up on the idea of bringing the championship back to its only location south of Lancashire, so that it could again become more accessible to golf followers from London and its neighbouring counties, the importance and value of the new development could not be exaggerated. Complaints surface from time to time about the standard and availability of the accommo-

Yawning bunkers, such as this at the fourth hole, are characteristic of Royal St George's.

dation nearby — although that is a perennial Open problem wherever it is played. The determination remained that this golfing outpost, comparatively isolated though it might be, should be encouraged to survive, and so it has, to the extent that it has been host now to three championships in 13 years, resurrection from a golfing graveyard if ever there was one.

The championship itself was willing to respond at once to this new lease of life by producing two winners, whose progress to the title and whose subsequent careers are in such stark opposition that the bystander could not but believe that, when the Open came back to Sandwich, old habits died hard. Although Bill Rogers had to overcome a brief crisis in the final round, his victory carried an authority that was never later substantiated. Sandy Lyle, on the other hand, crept up on the title almost unawares, as he did so leaving at least one disbelieving observer to remark: 'We are entering uncharted waters.' — not navigated, that is, since Tony Jacklin, 16 years before, enshrined himself as the last British winner.

For Rogers, then 30, the year of 1981 was indeed his *annus mirabilis*. On four continents he won seven events and more than US$500,000, very serious money indeed in those days. Having won on the US

PGA Tour in March, he gave advance warning in June of his potential for taking a major by finishing equal second to David Graham in the US Open at Merion. He duly triumphed at Sandwich — by four strokes from Bernhard Langer, having led by five strokes after three rounds — and again won five more times after that, twice back in America, subsequently in Japan and twice again in Australia, notably in that country's Open. In 1982 Rogers led with nine holes to play in the US Open at Pebble Beach, but was swept aside by Tom Watson's epic and victorious duel with Jack Nicklaus.

But Rogers ascendancy turned out to be as ephemeral as the starshell it so resembled. Seven years later — the boyish smile beneath the mophead of hair gone and his game and confidence undermined — Rogers departed the tournament grind. Since 1990 he has been the director of golf at the San Antonio Country Club in his native state of Texas, as remarkable an example of an idol fallen from grace as golf has known.

The lyricist who might have composed the phrase: 'Time hurries by, we're here and gone' with Rogers specifically in mind, would have had to think of a very different line for Lyle. A distinguished amateur career, 10 victories on the PGA European Tour, and

Bill Rogers (left) was the world's best in 1981, while Sandy Lyle (right) launched his championship career here in 1985.

three appearances in the Ryder Cup matches could not have been better preparation for winning an Open Championship. Later there would be a three-year spell barren of achievement. Fortune also favoured Lyle in 1985, for the draw protected him from the worst of the gale which afflicted the first two rounds, and he was in a challenging position with 18 holes to play.

Everyone remembers the agony of soul which Lyle revealed, and which was shared by the silenced thousands in the grandstands beside the home green, when his chip from Duncan's Hollow failed to crest the slope. In the end, all was well, but the shots which put Lyle into a winning position were at the 14th and 15th. At the 14th he hit a two iron more than 220 yards to the edge of the green and holed from 45 feet for the most improbable of birdie 4s, since he had hooked his drive into a wilderness. At the next, clearly inspired by that astounding advance, Lyle hit a huge drive and second shot to six feet for another birdie.

It was appropriate that it should be Lyle who restored spirits in the British camp after the title had 12 times crossed the Atlantic, once returned to South Africa, and twice, as a form of consolation and European solidarity, to Spain with Severiano Ballesteros.

Lyle's pedigree, if not his actual golfing pedigree, is as Scottish as was that of the principal founders of Royal St George's. When Scots were engaged in the Middle East on oil exploration work, it was said that they 'pitched a tent, drilled a well, and then laid out nine holes.' A similar philosophy, although not quite the same sequence of method, appears to have accompanied the prolonged efforts of Dr Laidlaw Purves to establish a links far removed physically and architecturally from what were rapidly becoming overcrowded courses in the London area.

A leading ophthalmic surgeon at Guy's Hospital, Purves also turned out to have a perceptive eye when the task of finding suitable land began. Something of an exploration followed, as Purves and Henry Lamb travelled the south coast of England without finding the place they sought to emulate the links tradition of their homeland, where St Andrews, Prestwick, North Berwick and Dornoch had become established as superior to any form of inland golf. The over-population on the courses at Wimbledon and Blackheath was rapidly growing intolerable, and the example set by the formation of the club at Westward Ho! in North Devon as the first English links was an added spur to them to persevere with their own search.

Just when it seemed as if the intrepid surveyors would run out of suitable possibilities and fail to have their patience rewarded, Purves, as the received account has it, climbed the Norman church tower of St Clements in the town of Sandwich, no act of penance or contrition, as it transpired, since once there he 'spied the land with a golfer's eye.' The untamed duneland lying between Sandwich and the English Channel, was precisely what they had their hearts and minds set on. Not only was the Earl of Guilford prepared to lease to them 300 of those wild acres, but the club was instituted, a course was built, and within only seven years, in 1894, it was deemed ready to host its first Open Championship — instant celebrity, indeed.

Every championship course has undergone some form of evolutionary process, as golf clubs and balls have changed character in material and manufacture, earth-moving machinery and agronomy have become more sophisticated, and, not least, opinion, expert and otherwise, has changed over what constitutes the best golfing challenge. St George's, which attained its regality in 1902, proved to be no exception to this rule although, according to no less an authority than Bernard Darwin, for some time it was arguable whether criticism of the course fell under the description of blasphemous or merely treasonable. Eventually, of course, the tide of events and the persuasiveness of the better-informed coalesced the conviction that changes were needed.

Central to the reservations about the original design of the course was the number of blind shots, caught in the vivid description of one writer in the last decade of the 19th century, Horace Hutchinson, that 'golf should not consist in hitting a shot over a sandhill and then running to the top of it to see where the ball has finished.' The modern architect is at pains to ensure that the humblest rabbit should at least be able to see where he is going, even if his sense of direction is not equalled by his ability to reach the desired destination. As well as a new road system, course alterations were made before 1981 to celebrate the championship's return to one of its roots.

The former versions of the third and 11th holes were replaced, more of the driving areas at the fourth and seventh were revealed, and part of the sand dune in front of the 14th tee was displaced so that the fairway became visible. All the same, the tee shots at Royal St George's are more rigorously examined than on most courses, particularly trying the patience of the professionals with the uneven lies and stances created by crumpled fairways, which often treat the most accurate drives with scant regard either for the player's reputation or for his mistaken presumption of the fairness factor.

The humps and hollows may not have created a lovely lie for a brassie — a club now as extinct as the stymie — but a century ago, when the total prize-money was £100, and the winner earned £30 of that, such niceties must have seemed just as minimal. Even so, professionals then had developed a sense of their own worth, not, obviously, pitched at anything like the levels of today. That did not, however, prevent some players in 1899 threatening to strike over their perception of the inadequacies of the purse. They had, it appears, no allies among the Great Triumvirate of Vardon, Taylor and James Braid, and St George's second Open proceeded to Vardon's successful defence.

Five years later White not only had a total of 296 but he was the first of still only four players — the others being Braid, Ben Hogan and Gary Player — to win with the score for each round lower than the one before. This achievement by a professional — and, incidentally, by one who was almost the first club professional the Honourable Company of Edinburgh Golfers has still never had — seemed to irk the perception of two of the day's foremost amateurs, Freddie Tait and Ted Blackwell, that carries from the tee could be as much as 150 yards, as well as being unsighted. The professionals are still playing a game with which even amateurs of the first rank are not by any stretch of the imagination familiar.

Since Vardon gained his fifth victory (of six) in 1911, when Arnaud Massy, seven strokes behind, conceded with one hole of their 36-hole play-off remaining, the Frenchman was equally out of his depth. Hagen's victory 11 years later was the first of four from only six attempts in eight years and, since he was second and third in the two others, his domi-

The distinctive starter's hut beside the first hole at Royal St George's.

nation of the Open Championships of the Jazz Age was complete. It was then left to Cotton, very different from Hagen in character and more fiercely dedicated to reaching the pinnacle and staying there, to staunch the haemorrageing of the championship to America. Royal St George's, in 1934, provided the stage on which Cotton disclosed the first of his three class acts.

Cotton's 65 in the second round was not improved upon for 43 years and his 36-hole total of 132 stood until as recently as last year, when Nick Faldo beat it by two strokes at Muirfield. The longevity of these records led one cynic to remark dismissively: 'Of course, golf doesn't get any better. It's like other sports, it's just attracted more money.' Since Cotton's prize was at the blunt end of three figures and the winner of this championship stretched between his fingers a cheque for £100,000, there might be some inclination to agree, not least by the last two winners before that long interregnum leading to the transformation of the game into the modern era.

In 1938 a gale devastating in its force afflicted the last day's play and, as the exhibition tent foundered like a dismasted schooner and everything from sweaters to golf clubs to sandwiches littered the surrounding countryside, Reg Whitcombe, one of only three players to break 80 in each of the last two rounds, stepped from the figurative lifeboat with a two-stroke victory. This represented a visit to the rock-face of the game compared with Locke's resounding triumph over Bradshaw in 1949, forever to be remembered for having hit a shot out of the debris of a broken bottle off the fifth fairway in the second round. Bradshaw decided to play the ball, as it lay, which he need not, of course, have done, and took 6, a double bogey.

If the genial Irishman had taken 4 he would not necessarily have tied — a cheerful, if unsupportable, assumption — since he would have had to play the remaining 49 holes in the same total of strokes and there could never be a guarantee on that score. Thus Locke took the £300 prize from a total of £1,700, the start of the period when, lacking serious and concerted overseas opposition, particularly from America, he and Peter Thomson dominated the Open with four victories each over 10 championships.

Gene Sarazen, now aged 91, was the first to win the modern Grand Slam, setting the standard for others.

THE REMARKABLE TIMES OF GENE SARAZEN

BY MICHAEL McDONNELL

One face in the crowd mattered more than perhaps all the rest and only afterwards could Greg Norman reflect how appropriate it was for this venerable gentleman to witness his accession to the title of Open champion at Royal St George's.

For the inescapable truth is that Gene Sarazen stands as the golfing giant against whom every aspiring champion must be judged, because he bestowed a set of unchangeable values on the game that will endure for as long as it is played.

Moreover, they are precepts that cannot be ignored, and all who have followed him — Ben Hogan, Jack Nicklaus, Gary Player and others — have measured their own greatness in varying degrees to the manner in which they have managed to emulate Sarazen's own exploits.

In a sense, therefore, Gene Sarazen set the shape, form and philosophy of professional golf as it is now conducted throughout the world. He gave the game a structure on which greatness could be based, and he did it by winning four championships that will forever be acknowledged as the most important in the game.

He is the man who invented the modern Grand Slam; the golfer who first won all four titles and that precedent, once set, had to be observed by those who sought to stand comparison with him. Indeed, it is a measure of the monumental task involved in winning that ultimate quartet of titles — the US Masters, the US Open, the Open and the USPGA Championship — that in the intervening 59 years only three other players have achieved it, and many great figures have been obliged to hang up their clubs one trophy short of the full collection.

Consequently, there is an inarguable completeness about the man who gains all four titles, not simply because he has acquired the 'full set,' but because he has demonstrated a comprehensive range of playing skills that can adapt to such diverse yet specific challenges.

If the links terrain of an Open Championship demands the traditional ability of imaginative shot-making, then the other three great events each present their own particular and identifiable examinations that collectively produce the complete champion. And perhaps it is a reflection of modern specialized talent that some champions can flourish only in certain, but not all, regions.

It means, of course, that whenever a new champion dons a green jacket or hoists one of the famous trophies aloft, the twinkling, puckish presence of Gene Sarazen will always pose the eternal question, 'Fine. Now how about the other three?'

In truth, such a doctrine has given the game itself a sense of order so that even champions themselves can be placed in certain categories of competence and importance by the range and number of major titles they have won.

The second doctrine of excellence that this dapper 91-year-old New Yorker laid upon professional golfers for all time is the most important of all because it ignores current transitory fashion and trends and instead adheres strictly to the only true manner in which a golfer's ability can be recognized and measured.

He says quite simply: 'At the end of your career, they don't ask how much money you won. They want to know how many majors did you win?' It is a nagging truth that no end of million-dollar contracts and top-10 finishes can assuage, and it had become a principle that taunted Greg Norman during that frustrating period of his life when he remained a top box office attraction yet could not deliver a commensurate number of major titles despite many well-documented near-misses.

It would have been unthinkable that a player of

Norman's talent might have gone through a playing career with his name engraved on only one major title, because that would have been insufficient reward for his skills and completely misrepresented his importance to future generations. Yet under the harsh implication of the Sarazen Principle he might well have remained in the margin of history.

Ironically, the same thing almost happened to Sarazen himself early in his career when, after a dynamic start in which he won two major titles in one season when still only 20 years old, he then disappeared from the company of champions for the best part of 10 years. Yet his greatest achievements were still ahead of him, and when he reappeared as a wiser and better player, he was to make history and secure his own chapter in the development of the game.

Eugene Saraceni was born of Italian immigrant stock in 1902, and lived in New York where he earned 45 cents a day as a caddie at a local golf club. He worked in the pro shop, repaired clubs and practised in every spare moment. He was self-educated but well-read. He was a courtly man with a penchant for plus-fours that were to become a trademark throughout his career and earned him the fond nickname of 'The Squire.'

He was a small man (5-ft-5) and could be abrasive and hot-tempered. He gave the ball an unmerciful lash and possessed a brimming confidence that, by his own admission, bordered on arrogance. Indeed, at one period of his life he toyed with the idea of a film star career in Hollywood after making a series of one-reel slapstick comedies, and had changed his name to Gene Sarazen.

He was therefore not in the least overawed by the reputations of the more famous stars around him when he arrived for the 1922 US Open at Skokie Country Club in Illinois, and had in fact visited the course a month earlier to plan his strategy. Yet the outcome — and his chance of success — was to depend essentially on the kind of spectacular match-winning stroke that was to become his hallmark. The Squire never backed off from a risky shot and sometimes paid a heavy price. But not this time.

He knew that Bobby Jones and other rivals were still out on the course as he came to the last hole and faced a massive stroke to the green with water on the left and out of bounds on the right. To play cautiously and lose was unthinkable, and he pondered for a moment then said to his caddie: 'Oh hell, give me the brassie.' The ball fizzed 12 feet from the flagstick and he was champion.

By the end of that year he had struck such rich form that he snapped up the USPGA Championship, then in its original match play form; and because Walter Hagen, the great hero of the day, had not played in that championship, went on to challenge The Haig to a lucrative and much-publicized 72-hole encounter, and beat him 3 and 2 before being whisked to hospital after the match for an emergency operation for appendicitis.

In career terms, however, the Open Championship was to prove extremely elusive and he made a succession of futile attempts, including a notorious failure in the 1928 contest at Royal St George's, when he ignored the advice of his local caddie and tried a miracle shot from the rough on the left of the 14th hole and ended up with a double-bogey 7 to lose the title by two strokes to — guess who? — Hagen himself.

There was a lifelong rivalry and respect between these two characters which spurred each to new heights of achievement, although Hagen was perceived as the established hero under constant challenge from Sarazen, whom he irritated by calling 'Kid' and over whom he always seemed to have a psychological edge. When Sarazen was playing the last round of that 1928 Open, he was suddenly aware that Hagen who had finished earlier had come back on the course to watch him play the closing holes ... in the company of the Prince of Wales.

The frustration for Sarazen was that his contemporaries — Jones, Hagen and company — seemed able to pick off the Open title almost at will, but he kept missing out and admitted later: 'After I failed a couple of times I developed such a complex about this championship that my subsequent attempts took on the emotional overcharged proportions of a crusade. But I said I would be back even if I had to swim.'

It almost came to that, because Sarazen lost most of his investments in the Wall Street crash of 1929 and did not have the money to travel to Prince's for the 1932 Open until his wife revealed that she had bought him the boat tickets. Thus it was that a wiser and more complete golfer arrived at the Kent course to be reunited eventually with the old caddie whose advice he had ignored so ruinously five years earlier.

He was not only more accomplished but better equipped, too. He had come to the conclusion that his bunker play was so weak that it had affected his confidence in the rest of his game, because he simply did not have the skill with the thin-edged niblick to pick the ball from the sand.

Accordingly, he decided to build a wing-like flange on the back of the club so that it came into contact with the sand while the leading edge remained raised and popped the ball free. In fact, not only had he invented the sand wedge, but Sarazen had also devised the explosion shot and became so adept that he could guarantee to get up and down from any sand trap.

Even so, when he arrived at Prince's for the 1932 championship, he decided to keep his new club a closely guarded secret until the event began just in case the Championship Committee chose to disapprove, as they had done with the Walter Travis centre-shafted Shenactedy putter. However, there were no such repercussions, even when he began to demonstrate an extraordinary wizardry with the wedge-shaped club from the sand traps of Prince's.

He led all the way to finish on 283 and beat the Open record set by Bobby Jones at St Andrews in 1927 when he scored 285. But more importantly, he had curbed his compulsion to take risks and instead relied so completely on the judgement of his faithful caddie that he asked if the old retainer could join him at the prize-giving ceremony. The request was tactfully refused.

No matter. It was to be the start of a historic revival in his career in which he travelled back across the Atlantic and with only a week to spare still found a level of form good enough to win the US Open title with a last round 66 at Fresh Meadows Country Club in New York which included a classic bunker shot with his new-fangled club to save par on the 18th hole and finish clear of his rivals.

A year later he won his third USPGA title, but there was still one important victory to be secured, although it is arguable now whether the US Masters at the time had achieved the status of a major championship, even though all the great players of the era turned up to play on a course that had been designed by Bobby Jones to test them to their limits.

Whatever else, the US Masters — or rather Augusta National itself — provided another moment for match-winning artistry when on the final day in 1935 Craig Wood was already in the clubhouse being acknowledged as the winner of the second Masters Tournament until he heard a roar from the depths of the course.

It signalled one of the most remarkable strokes in history, as Sarazen holed a full four-wood shot on the long 15th across the water for a double-eagle 2 that was to lift him into an eventual tie with Wood and a 36-hole play-off the next day, which he won with 144 to his rival's 149. Thus he had acquired the complete set of titles, although he had to wait another 14 years before he could wear a green jacket because that practice was not adopted until 1949.

For Sarazen, there was nothing left to prove, and he never won another major title, although even in retirement he still revived memories of his great ability to strike the most sensational shots. At the age of 71 in the 1973 Open, he holed his tee shot at the Postage Stamp on Royal Troon and on the following day sank a bunker shot on the same hole for a birdie.

For sheer longevity, the life and times of Gene Sarazen are remarkable enough, but it is the measure of a truly great man that aspects of his life — either separate or collectively — give inspiration to others. And if Greg Norman really was tormented by the Sarazen maxim that only major titles matter, then he could also be uplifted by the thought that even the Grand Old Man of Golf had hoisted himself out of 10 years of decline to find that even greater glories were awaiting him. That was the most important message of all, because it offered a reason never to stop trying.

Greg Norman started with a double-bogey 6, but recovered with eight birdies, including five in succession.

NORMAN, THREE OTHERS HAVE 66

BY ROBERT SOMMERS

At the height of its power, when the British Empire encircled the globe, men said an Englishman walks the earth as if he owned it. Whoever made such an observation obviously had not watched Peter Senior walk a golf course in full pursuit of the Open Championship. A short, blocky Australian with a squarish face, a glorious moustache and a seemingly permanent scowl, Senior strides the earth not so much as if he owns it but as if whoever does may take title only when he is through using it.

As one of the early starters in the first round of the 1993 championship, Senior used the Royal St George's Golf Club very well indeed, ripping around in 66 and becoming the first of four men to shade par by four strokes and share the 18-hole lead. Senior was followed quickly by the American Mark Calcavecchia, the 1989 champion, who began only 20 minutes behind him, and then by Greg Norman, a fellow Australian, who had won at Turnberry in 1986. Later in the day Fuzzy Zoeller, the 1984 US Open champion, fired 66 as well.

All of this turned out to be a surprising turn of events, for situated on England's southeastern coast, where unpredictable can be the kindest description of weather coming from off the English Channel, Royal St George's can be the most severe test on the Open rota. Furthermore, with England gripped by a determined drought — rainfall for the previous seven weeks so slight it couldn't be measured — predictions indicated a high-scoring championship in which a parred hole would stand as a measure of excellence.

Peter Senior was one of four with 66.

In the days leading up to the championship, the 122nd, by the way, the players talked quite cautiously of what they might expect. On the eve of the first round, Nick Faldo, defending the championship that had wracked him so emotionally when he won it a year earlier, pointed to the dry and bouncy condition of the fairways and predicted the Open could be won with a score over the par of 280, as Sandy Lyle had done in 1985, the last championship over this ancient ground.

Faldo, and everyone agreed, rated Royal St George's as the toughest on the rota, purely because of the conditions — the lack of rain and the perpetual wind whipping across the great dunes. He called it the firmest course since Royal Troon four years earlier, 'Maybe the firmest I've played. The downwind holes will play very short, but that doesn't mean they'll be easy; you have to stop the ball. With the bounces, this will be very tricky. Having a wedge in your hand doesn't mean you have an easy chance at a birdie.'

All that was speculation, for the players faced different conditions once the championship began. Rain fell Tuesday night and again Wednesday, then more rain soaked Royal St George's Thursday. Pathways throughout the tented village and alongside the fairways, where spectators were forced to follow the play, oozed mud, turning walking into a hazardous exercise. One spectator slipped and lay in the muck alongside the ninth hole with a suspected broken ankle. Others were seen sliding off hummocks to undignified landings. Greens once hard

William Guy of Scotland led off the 122nd Open Championship at 7.15 am.

1989 champion Mark Calcavecchia had 66 with no bogeys.

Fuzzy Zoeller, also with 66, said he drove well.

Larry Mize (67) saved par at the 15th and 17th.

Howard Clark (67) was putting back-handed.

as bricks that had rejected even the well-hit shot during practice rounds had turned soft and forgiving.

In its years out of the rota, Royal St George's had been criticized for its capricious character. Well-struck balls bounced erratically over the rolling, tumbling dunes, often kicking into the knee-high rough lining the generous fairways. No more. Under the changed conditions the players were able to control their shots.

Consequently the field turned in unusually low scores. Where in 1985 only 10 men had broken par during the first round, 47 shot under 70 and another 22 matched par — 69 men at par or better. In addition to the four who shot 66, another 10 shot 67, and 14 more shot 68.

Bernhard Langer, who had won his second US Masters earlier in the year, was among those at 67, along with Larry Mize, who had won the 1987 US Masters. Fred Couples, who blazed home in 32, and Nick Price, playing at the top of his game, each were among those at 68, and after a blistering 32 going out, Faldo stumbled home in 37 and matched Lee Janzen, the current US Open champion, at 69.

Some old and favoured names played some of their best golf of recent years. Seve Ballesteros, for ex-

ample, reached into what might be a dwindling reserve and shot 68, and Jack Nicklaus, encouraged by winning the US Senior Open only four days earlier, shot 69, along with 18 others.

Judging from his history, Greg Norman must not have felt particularly comfortable as he looked around at those tied with him after the first round; all three had beaten him in important competitions. Zoeller had thumped him badly in a play-off for the 1984 US Open, and Calcavecchia had beaten him in another play-off for the 1989 Open Championship when Greg had thrown away a one-stroke lead by bogeying Royal Troon's 17th and then driving into a fairway bunker on the 18th, allowing Calcavecchia to win with a birdie 3.

That leaves Peter Senior. Norman lost the 1991 Australian Masters to Senior when Greg hooked his drive to the last hole at the Huntingdale Golf Club, in Melbourne, behind a three-tiered hospitality complex. Norman pitched his ball so far over the obstruction it hit a similar structure on the opposite side of the green, bounced off, and skittered back across the green and into a bunker. Senior beat him by one stroke.

Squat and powerful at 5-ft-5, just a little taller than Ian Woosnam, Senior walks the fairways with his

Greg Turner shot 67 despite a double bogey.

Wayne Westner (67) said he liked to play links courses.

Mark McNulty (67) birdied two of the last three holes.

eyes straight ahead, muscular arms pumping, and moustache bristling. Like the juggernaut rolling over everything in its path, Senior gives the distinct impression of the irresistible force that will crush the immovable object.

He has a swing that is uniquely his own. Drawing the club back in an orthodox manner, he comes into the ball with a decided upward lurch, as if he has suddenly realized the club may be a little too long for him and he must compensate by raising himself higher.

He also uses the long putter, a club given to him five years ago by Sam Torrance, another disciple of the system. Senior holds the butt of the shaft under his chin with his left hand and strokes the ball with his right hand well down the shaft.

Peter can be sensitive about the putter.

'Some days when I hole a lot of putts everyone thinks I'm cheating. They don't say that when I'm putting badly. If you finish 50th every week, they're not going to say anything.'

By the time Senior teed off, at 8.20, under dull gray clouds and threats of further rain, the scoreboard already showed sprinklings of red numbers, indicating holes played under par, a clear warning of what lay ahead.

After saving his par on the first by holing a nerve-wracking eight-footer, Senior began his assault by pitching to 15 feet on the second and rolling the putt home for a birdie 3. Two more pars brought him to the fifth, the hole where John Daly had driven the green in a practice round and where Harry Bradshaw had played a ball lying inside a broken bottle during the 1949 Open. Daly had flown his drive over the left hump that rises at about the distance of a good drive by anyone else.

Taking a more sensible approach, Senior laid up short of the humps with his two iron, then played a four iron inside 15 feet and holed the putt for his second birdie. Two more pars, one a missed birdie chance when his putt from eight feet skimmed past the cup on the sixth, brought him to the eighth hole, a par 4 of 418 yards. A drive and another four iron left him 30 feet from the cup, and, behold, the long putter worked — he rolled it in.

Des Smyth (67) felt he could 'get away with a few bad shots.'

Except for one drive, Bernhard Langer (67) said he played solidly.

Three under par now, Senior ripped another drive down the middle and laid a nine iron 25 feet away on the ninth. Once again the long putter did its job, a second straight birdie, his fourth of the first nine. Senior had gone out in 31, matching Henry Cotton's outgoing score in 1934. Cotton had followed with 34 on the incoming nine, but such a score stood out of Senior's reach. A mis-played approach putt on the 11th, a par 3 of 216 yards, cost him a bogey, and he could pick up only one birdie, holing a 10-foot putt on the 13th, a strong par 4 of 443 yards, close to Pegwell Bay, which skirts the outer reaches of the course.

Senior came home in even-par 35, managing to par every one of those strong finishing holes and missing only the 15th green, where he holed a 15-foot putt for his 4.

By the time Senior finished, Larry Mize, playing the best golf he had ever shown in an Open, had already posted 67, and both Iain Pyman, the Amateur champion, and Jesper Parnevik, the Swede who had won the Bell's Scottish Open the previous week, were in with 68, and Paul Azinger had shot 69.

Then, within 20 minutes, Calcavecchia came in with his own 66, and 10 minutes later Norman stormed home with his own.

Finding Calcavecchia among the leaders surprised most spectators; Mark hadn't been at his best since he won the 1989 Open, the last American champion. His career reached its lowest point, perhaps, during the 1991 Ryder Cup match, in South Carolina, when he held Colin Montgomerie four down with four to play and lost every hole, including the 17th, a long par 3 over water, even though Montgomerie hit his tee shot into the lake. Calcavecchia hit two into the water.

Calcavecchia blamed his putting for his fall from the game's heights, saying it had turned sour as a bowl of old milk. Home in Arizona, he owns at least 75 putters, and then, in April, he bought his 76th, spending US$45 to buy it. It has worked well for him ever since.

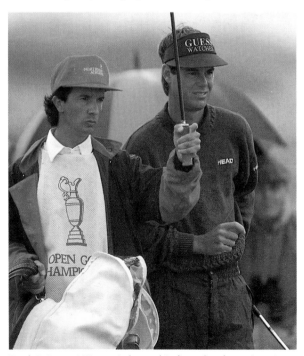

Paul Azinger (69) carried over his fine play from America.

Lee Janzen (69) had no trouble on the greens.

Greg Norman holed a 15-foot putt at the 18th to finish his 66, four under par.

Grouped with Faldo and Steve Elkington, Calcavecchia holed from 15 feet on the second, and from four feet to save par on the fourth. Another birdie at the seventh, at 530 yards the longest of the two par 5s, and Calcavecchia was out in 33.

The trip home held more perils as the wind began to rise and rain fell seriously for a time. Off quickly with birdies on the 10th and 12th, Mark worked his way through the Trinity, that dangerous stretch of holes beginning at the 13th and ending with the 15th, then missed the 16th green. A pitch to two feet saved par there, and his approach to the 17th rolled 60 feet from the cup, a dangerous distance. With renewed confidence in his putting, Calcavecchia rolled it close and made his par.

Another par on the 18th, and he strutted off the final green with a blemish-free 66, played without bogeying one hole.

Norman couldn't make a similar claim, and, in fact, played a much more erratic round. He began with a poor drive into the deep rough, tried to reach the green with an eight iron and failed, took two more shots before hitting the green, and two-putted from nine feet. A double-bogey 6.

Norman was stunned, of course, but not beaten yet. He told himself he had 71 more holes to play, and he should make some birdies and work his way back to even par. He did. A three wood and sand wedge to 18 feet on the second earned one, and then a four iron and six iron to nine feet on the fifth earned the second.

Another bogey on the sixth followed by a birdie on the seventh brought him to the nine-hole turn in 35, even par. Another bogey at the 11th, where he missed the green. Now he stood one over par with the most demanding holes coming up. A par at the 12th, as close as Royal St George's comes to a birdie hole, and then Norman was off on one of the championship's great bursts of scoring.

A great pitch to 18 inches at the 13th brought Greg back to even par, and then he had a great break. His third shot missed the 14th green, but from 45 feet he holed a sand wedge.

One under par now, Norman drilled a six iron within two feet on the 15th for his third consecutive birdie, and followed up by holing a putt from 24 feet on the 16th. Four consecutive birdies, and now Greg stood at three under par. He had made up five strokes after his opening double bogey.

Still, he wasn't through. He drove well on the 17th, and on that difficult hole ripped a five iron within five feet. Another putt fell — a fifth consecutive birdie.

Four under par now, Norman missed the 18th green, but he holed from 15 feet to save par. Playing a series of sensational irons through that scoring stretch and putting like a dream over a very difficult series of holes, Norman had come back in 31 and finished with 66.

The question remained, though, whether or not he could hold up. He had played sensational rounds in the past, and yet fallen out of the chase with a

Sam Torrance (72) had spasms in his shoulder.

Ian Woosnam (72) struggled in the first round.

Amateur champion Iain Pyman (68) played well tee to green.

championship at stake.

With scores such as this so early in the day (when Norman teed off at 9 o'clock, more than 90 percent of the field still had to play), nearly everyone anticipated even more lower scoring as the day progressed. Those who counted on it were disappointed, for only Zoeller matched those early 66s, although nostalgic passions rose with the showings of both Nicklaus and Ballesteros.

To call Seve's reappearance among the game's elite nostalgic may seem to stretch a point, for he is only 36, but nevertheless he has been in a deep slump for several years, and he had struggled through a series of high scores in the 1993 season. Ballesteros himself admitted his pleasure with his position.

Playing two groups behind Ballesteros, Nicklaus too opened as if he were still in his prime, with two birdies in the first three holes, and after stumbling over the fourth and fifth, bogeying both, he played the last 13 holes in one under par. This was his best first round in the Open since 1977, when he and Tom Watson battled through four stirring rounds at Turnberry. But Jack had nothing left. This championship was left to younger men.

Favourites Jose Maria Olazabal (left, 73) and Davis Love III (right, 70) would miss the 36-hole cut.

Three-times champion Jack Nicklaus (69) had an encouraging start, but also failed to qualify.

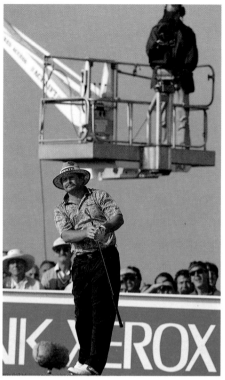

Photographers, television cameramen and writers documented the 122nd Open Championship.

FIRST ROUND RESULTS

HOLE	1	2	3	4	5	6	7	8	9	10	11	12	13	14	15	16	17	18	
PAR	4	4	3	4	4	3	5	4	4	4	3	4	4	5	4	3	4	4	TOTAL
Peter Senior	4	3	3	4	3	3	5	3	3	4	4	4	3	5	4	3	4	4	66
Mark Calcavecchia	4	3	3	4	4	3	4	4	4	3	3	3	4	5	4	3	4	4	66
Greg Norman	6	3	3	4	3	4	4	4	4	4	4	4	3	4	3	2	3	4	66
Fuzzy Zoeller	3	4	4	3	4	3	4	4	3	4	3	3	4	5	4	3	4	4	66
Larry Mize	4	4	3	4	3	3	4	3	3	4	3	5	4	5	4	3	4	4	67
Greg Turner	4	4	3	6	4	2	4	3	4	3	3	4	4	4	4	2	5	4	67
Gary Evans	3	4	3	4	4	2	4	4	4	4	3	3	4	5	4	3	5	4	67
Mark McNulty	4	4	3	4	4	3	5	4	4	3	3	4	4	5	4	2	4	3	67
Howard Clark	4	4	3	4	4	3	4	4	4	3	3	4	3	4	4	3	5	4	67
Des Smyth	5	4	2	4	5	3	4	3	4	4	3	4	4	4	2	4	4	4	67
Bernhard Langer	4	3	3	4	4	3	4	4	4	3	3	4	4	4	4	3	4	4	67
Wayne Westner	4	4	3	4	4	2	5	4	4	4	3	3	4	5	4	2	4	4	67
Glen Day	5	3	3	4	4	3	4	4	4	4	3	4	3	4	3	3	5	4	67
Stephen Ames	3	4	3	5	4	2	4	4	4	4	3	4	5	4	4	2	4	4	67

HOLE SUMMARY

HOLE	PAR	EAGLES	BIRDIES	PARS	BOGEYS	HIGHER	RANK	AVERAGE
1	4	0	16	103	33	4	5	4.16
2	4	0	25	119	10	2	15	3.93
3	3	0	15	103	37	1	3	3.17
4	4	0	6	82	57	11	1	4.49
5	4	0	16	122	16	2	13	4.03
6	3	0	19	108	27	2	11	3.08
7	5	5	95	53	3	0	18	4.35
8	4	0	19	99	36	2	7	4.13
9	4	0	22	106	27	1	12	4.04
OUT	35	5	233	895	246	25		35.38
10	4	0	16	108	29	3	9	4.12
11	3	0	11	118	27	0	6	3.10
12	4	0	18	118	19	1	14	4.02
13	4	0	18	106	29	3	10	4.11
14	5	0	43	95	14	4	17	4.88
15	4	0	14	113	24	5	7	4.13
16	3	0	30	106	19	1	16	2.94
17	4	0	12	100	43	1	4	4.21
18	4	0	10	94	48	4	2	4.30
IN	35	0	172	958	252	22		35.81
TOTAL	70	5	405	1853	498	47		71.19

			LOW SCORES		
Players Below Par	47				
Players At Par	22		Low First Nine	Larry Mize	31
				Peter Senior	31
Players Above Par	87		Low Second Nine	Greg Norman	31
			Low Round	Mark Calcavecchia	66
				Greg Norman	66
				Peter Senior	66
				Fuzzy Zoeller	66

Seve Ballesteros has been Britain's adopted golfing son, one with the charisma of Arnold Palmer.

BRITAIN'S ADOPTED SON

BY MICHAEL WILLIAMS

Somewhere along the line the magic had dimmed. But his public had not forgotten. They were gathering around the first tee well before 2 o'clock on that Thursday afternoon and when at 2.10, under police escort from the close-at-hand practice green he finally appeared to set his face to the challenge of the next four days, the warmth of the reception he received was enough to bring a tear to the eye.

Severiano Ballesteros, or just Seve now to the world, may be Spanish but he has long been Britain's adopted golfing son, even perhaps its favourite son. No one, not even Nick Faldo, who is everything British and has passed just as many of the game's toughest examinations as Seve, has commanded such a following. The charisma Ballesteros has generated over the years has been no less than that of Arnold Palmer in the United States.

There are, of course, similarities. Neither has ever been conservative in his approach to the game. Both have been attacking players, Palmer the roaring lion with his vast hands enveloping the handle of the club and pouring such venom into his shots that he often rebounds out of the top of the upswing, Ballesteros the panther with his poise and balance as everything blends together into a gloriously full and flowing swing that comes only with a natural genius for the game.

Just to see his set-up immediately before he begins to take the club away is enough to tell the watcher that here is someone who can play golf. Everything, from the grip to the stance, is in place and he is one of the few players I know whom other players, when they have finished, have gone out to watch.

For one so perfect there have conversely been countless shots which have ended up in the wrong parish. They called him indeed the 'car park champion' when he won the first of his three Open Championships at Royal Lytham in 1979, for his drive at the 16th in the final round had come to rest beneath a car in a parking lot. But he still pitched and putted for his birdie 3.

Nor was that the only misdirected missile. Hale Irwin was Ballesteros' partner that day but the only times they met were on the tees and greens. While Irwin was hitting it down the middle, the Spaniard was repeatedly up to his eyes in hay but still somehow coming out on to the green where he would hole the putt. Bemused, Irwin could only produce a white handkerchief of surrender as he came to the 18th green.

With each of these dazzling recoveries Ballesteros would produce an equally dazzling smile. It was enough to melt the hearts of many a maiden, and the young man who could hardly speak a word of English when in 1976 he had tied second to Johnny Miller at Royal Birkdale had developed such a mastery of the language that he can deflate even the most loaded question by the probing interviewer.

Ballesteros was only 19 when he was runner-up to Miller, but the low chip he played between two bunkers at the last hole had such imagination and touch that even then it was seen to be a shot that would echo around the world. The reverberations have been going on ever since, or at least until this summer of 1993.

Until then Ballesteros had won at least one tournament every year. His first had come only a week after that Birkdale Open of 1976, in Holland, and his accumulation worldwide since then had risen to 68, three of them Open Championships, two of them US Masters. As recently as 1991 he had topped the PGA European Tour's Order of Merit for the sixth time, though the first signs of a decline were there in 1992. Though he had won twice, the Dubai Desert Classic and the Turespana Open, he had slipped to 28th place in the Order of Merit and that was his worst since his rookie year in 1974.

The 1993 season had begun promisingly enough

Ballesteros has won every year since 1976.

with third place in Dubai, but little had gone right since. In his next 10 European tournaments he had missed the cut five times and had not finished higher than 23rd in any of them. He was consequently 68th in the money list, while in the Sony Ranking, which once he had led, he had dropped to 23rd, 10 places worse than he had been at the beginning of the year. Almost the only flicker had been 11th equal in the US Masters, but when the US Open came along at Baltusrol he had missed the cut again, by four strokes.

It was hard to bear, not only for Ballesteros, but also for his followers who, with that British loyalty for a man who is down on his luck, were fairly willing him to succeed as he stood that Thursday afternoon gazing down the humpback first fairway at Sandwich. If it brought a lump to his throat, it also brought some of the old bounce to his game as well. He was bunkered at the first but he came out to eight feet and sank the putt to save par. It was, he reflected, as important a shot or putt as he played all day.

He missed the third green on the left but chipped to three feet and saved par again. He was left again at the fifth, where the green for the second shot is hidden beyond a saddle of dunes, chipped to 10 feet and once more par was saved.

Ballesteros' first birdie came at the seventh, a par 5. In relation to par this was to prove the easiest hole on the course with an average of 4.35 for the four days. Ballesteros was on with a drive and two iron and two-putted from 15 feet. He sank a putt of similar length for another birdie at the ninth after a nine-iron second and he was out in 33.

At last the putter was responding and he moved to three under at the drive-and-pitch 12th with a long putt after a nine iron had suggested a par to be the more likely. He was on the leaderboards now and after 14 holes he was four under par and tying the lead. Again the birdie was more reminiscent of the past than the present, for Ballesteros had dragged his two-iron second into the rough short and left of the green. A bunker was between him and the flag but he played it beautifully to four feet and in the putt went again.

An air of forgotten expectancy hung over the links now. Just one more birdie and he would be in front on his own. Instead, there were two bogeys and what could have been became what might have been. A hook from the 17th tee left him in the hay and it took him two more heaves with the nine iron to reach the green from where he two-putted for a 5.

At the 18th he was wide of the fairway again, this time on the right. The lie was better than at the previous hole but a five iron could not quite reach the green. However, he pitched to six feet, only this time to miss the putt. A 68 nonetheless and, as Ballesteros put it when he arrived for the post-round interview, 'I felt 15 years younger out there today.'

His mood was buoyant. 'If I can play three more rounds like that, I think I have a chance,' he said. 'I played more consistently today. I drove my ball very well, my short game was excellent and my putting was very good and that is why I scored well.'

What helped in particular had been those early putts to save par and then making birdies at the seventh and ninth. 'When you get some birdies it is easier to breathe,' he pondered. 'It gives you the chance to make some bogeys and still you are there. You give yourself some room and feel very young again. When you start making bogeys, you feel very old.

'It was very nice to go to the first tee and have such a brave reception. I still have a lot of loyal fans even though I have not been playing very well. Everyone encouraged me a lot all the way. My good round today was thanks to the people.'

Ballesteros said he had begun to feel more comfortable with his swing the night before. His problems, he admitted, had been of a technical nature, a lot of them in the mind. He has not been short of advice, for everyone wants to help. Perhaps indeed too many.

One thinks today of Faldo and David Leadbetter or Jack Nicklaus and, when he was alive, Jack Grout. Every spring Nicklaus used to go for a tuning up with Grout for here was a man who knew his pupil from his earliest days. He was like a doctor with the case history of a patient he had known since birth, not some general practitioner poking around for the first time.

Often, with a player-coach relationship like the one Tom Kite has with Harvey Penick, whose *Little Red Book* has become a best-seller, all the player has to do is pick up the telephone and describe the shots that are causing him trouble. Penick, because he knows Kite so well, can locate the fault without even seeing the swing.

Ballesteros does not have that relationship. Even though he has brothers who themselves are professional golfers, he was still self-taught. As a boy in Pedrena, he used to carve his own golf clubs from the driftwood lying on the beach and find the roundest stones he could to hit as golf balls. Sometimes, even at dead of night, he would slip out from the sleeping household and practise on the beach by moonlight. Augusta meant nothing to him then, nor the silver claret jug he has since

Ballesteros remains self-taught.

won three times as Open champion.

Ballesteros was a man who worked out his own salvation. He was a golfer of instinct, one who was born, not made. His first club was a three iron and he could do anything with it, even soft little bunker shots around the green. If ever there was a one-club tournament, Ballesteros would be the man.

It is less the case now that he has 14 clubs in his bag and, as Ballesteros followed that 68 with rounds of 73, 69 and 71 for 281 and equal 27th place, there was even uncertainty that he would make the Ryder Cup he himself had re-built over the previous 14 years.

It was because of him that a team previously made up of players from Britain and Ireland was extended to the continent of Europe. That was in 1979 and his very presence, his love of man-to-man combat, his leadership and ability to lift others to new heights had turned a historically one-sided match into a much more even one.

He it was who holed the putt that gave Europe its first victory in America in 1987, he whose constant presence around the course encouraging others after he had finished that had helped to inspire the victory of 1985 and the tie of 1989, both times at The Belfry.

But time marches on for every man, and Ballesteros once suggested that he might have played too much golf, begun at too early an age and was finding now that the batteries were running dry. Who knows? He is not old at 36, the same age at which Ben Hogan won the first of his four US Open Championships and the second of his USPGAs. A second coming is by no means beyond the bounds of possibility for Ballesteros.

'There is no such thing as a perfect round,' said Nick Faldo, whose 63 for a 132 total was close to it.

FALDO EQUALS THE RECORD

BY ROBERT SOMMERS

Even though he stood three strokes behind the co-leaders after the first 18 holes, Nick Faldo's presence caused everyone else to feel apprehensive. Going into the Open Championship it was generally agreed the final result depended on how well he played. The most dangerous player in the game, he had accumulated an astonishing record in the competitions that matter most, a record that rivalled those of the great players of the past.

Since he broke through at Muirfield six years earlier, Nick not only had won the Open twice more — at St Andrews in 1990 and at Muirfield again in 1992 — he had won the US Masters twice, lost a play-off for the 1988 US Open, placed third in the 1990 US Open, missing a place in the play-off with Hale Irwin and Mike Donald by one stroke, and tied for second in the 1992 USPGA Championship.

His record in the Open stands out above his performance in every other important competition. Through 1992 he had played in 17, dating back to 1976, when he was still in his teens, and he had never missed the cut, remarkable of itself. Even with his old loose, floppy swing, he had placed as high as seventh back in 1978, and during one exceptional period, from 1982 through 1984, he placed fourth, eighth and sixth, and then fifth in 1986, the year Greg Norman won at Turnberry.

Since revitalizing his swing, Faldo had won three Opens, and placed third in 1988 while Seve Ballesteros and Nick Price waged their inspiring battle at

Caddie Peter Coleman and Bernhard Langer.

Royal Lytham and St Annes, which Ballesteros finally won on the 72 green. Over Nick's entire Open career, which comprised 68 rounds of golf, he had played 24 rounds in the 60s, fully 35 percent, and shot his lowest round in 1992, 64 in the second round, which thrust him to the front, a position he never gave up until he played some loose golf early in the second nine of the last round. Still, he had won out in the end.

This perseverance, this determination, this refusal to be beaten elevated Faldo to a higher lever. He intimidated his rivals, and when once again he played a sensational second round at Royal St George's, a nearly flawless 63 that matched the Open record and shot him into the lead, it was clear the championship was his to either win or lose.

Heavy rain had struck the channel coast Thursday night, further weakening Royal St George's defences. The wind rose stronger for the late starters, blustering across some fairways, down others, and into the shot on still more, giving the field a better taste of what golf along the English Channel can be like. Although scoring did not reach the levels of the first round, 26 men shot rounds in the 60s, not as many as the 47 who had broken par a day earlier, but when the day ended the best players in the game stood at the top of the standings. In the lead position, Faldo was being challenged by Bernhard Langer, Fred Couples, Greg Norman, Corey Pavin, Peter Senior, Fuzzy Zoeller and Larry Mize.

An early starter on Thursday, Faldo was to play

Surprising even himself, Fred Couples shot 66–134.

in the afternoon on Friday. By the time he arrived, low scores had already been turned in. The day had hardly begun when Couples, who had opened with 68 on Thursday, birdied the second and third and dropped to four under par for the 21 holes. By the time he had played the fifth, Langer had birdied the first. The field was off to another day of great scoring.

Couples remains an enigma, an outstanding golfer who shows very little drive. Fred projects the impression he is essentially lazy and indifferent to practice, and has a low confidence level. He said he had come into the championship without much faith in his ability to win, and admitted he had actually given himself very little chance against Faldo, Norman and Price.

Nevertheless, Couples suddenly threatened to claim the lead. After routine pars on the fourth to the sixth, where he missed a birdie opportunity from six feet, Couples rifled two big shots to the edge of the seventh green, chipped to two feet, and holed the putt for another birdie.

Three under par for the day now, and five under for 25 holes, Couples bogeyed the eighth, but quickly floated a nine iron three feet from the cup on the ninth. Out in 32, four under par, Couples had dipped six under par for 27 holes and had taken over first place. Better things lay ahead.

Two missed greens but superb recoveries saved pars on the 10th and 11th, and then Couples reeled off three consecutive birdies, one of the miracle type. A long and pure drive left him in prime position for his approach to the 12th, but he made a tentative, cautious pass at his pitch and left it at least 40 feet short of the cup. No matter, Fred drew back his putter and gave the ball a good rap. It ran true to the hole and dived in for a 3.

When the putt fell, Couples rolled his eyes heavenward, turned toward the applauding gallery, and while his jaw dropped, he held out his hands, palms upward, as if to say he was more amazed than anyone.

He followed with a terrific pitch inside 10 feet on the 13th, reached the green of the 14th with a drive and a 225-yard three wood into the wind and birdied once again.

44

While Greg Norman worked on his 68-134, wife Laura (right) got some refreshments along the way.

His only bad shot, said Corey Pavin (66-134), was into this bunker at the 16th, where he saved par.

Peter Senior (69-135) made par from eight feet at the 16th after a fine bunker shot.

In sunglasses, Fuzzy Zoeller shot 70-136.

Now he stood six under par for the round, eight under for 32 holes. Safely past the dangerous 15th, Fred played a superb eight iron that pulled up eight feet from the cup, offering the opening to drop to nine under. The putt slipped past the cup, a lost opportunity.

Now Couples had reached that demanding finish, two tough par 4s, perhaps the most severe finish in the game. They ruined Fred's day. He missed the 17th green when his two iron pulled up 20 feet short and right, then pulled another two iron left of the home green, leaving it in the depression where Sandy Lyle had found himself at the finish of the 1985 Open. Here Couples chipped his ball across the green and bogeyed. With a round of 64 in reach, he had finished in 66 instead, and posted 134 for 36 holes, six under par, solidly among the leaders.

Meantime, Langer continued to play sound, error-free golf, reeling off three birdies on the first nine and making the turn in 32. When he began the second nine with a par 4 he had played 28 holes with nothing but 3s and 4s. He broke the string at the 11th, drilling a four iron to just over 15 feet and with his weird putting grip, ran the ball home for a birdie 2.

Another birdie at the 14th, where, realizing he couldn't reach the green with his second, he drove

46

Larry Mize (136) had bogeys at the 17th and 18th.

Peter Baker (137) birdied two of the last three holes.

with a one iron, played another one iron short, then pitched within eight feet and holed the putt for his final birdie of the day.

Now he stood five under par, on his way to a round of 65 and a 36-hole score of 132, eight under par, but he still had to face that dangerous finish. A drive and seven iron put him safely on the 15th for a routine par, and then another routine par on the 16th. Now for the 17th, 425 yards but playing much longer than it measured. A drive, then another one iron, hit as well as he had ever hit one, reached the green, and he two-putted from 60 feet.

One hole to go, the long and forbidding 18th, 468 yards into the wind. Reaching for all the distance he could muster, Langer hit his drive among the gallery and struck a woman. She wasn't hurt badly, but now Bernhard couldn't reach the green with his second. He bogeyed, his first 5 and only his second bogey. (He had made 4 on the 16th on Thursday.)

Langer finished with 66, which matched Couples' round, but with 133, he stood one stroke ahead of Fred over the distance.

None of that mattered very much, for Faldo was about to redefine the championship with one of the Open's greatest rounds, 63, that carried him to the top of the standings and created a new atmosphere.

John Daly (137) used his driver on 13 holes.

Nick had been accused of playing too conservatively in the past, playing for the certain par rather than risking a stroke with a daring shot. Perhaps, but there was nothing tentative or cautious about this round.

Six strokes behind Langer when he stepped on to the first tee, Faldo played daring, attacking golf from the first blow. Driving the fairway, Nick ripped a perfectly played five iron to four feet and holed the putt for the first of his seven birdies. One stroke closer.

He followed with two routine pars, then played a two-iron approach that missed the fourth green. After a six-iron chip, he saved himself by holing a nerve-testing four-footer.

Now Faldo reeled off three consecutive birdies. A safe three-iron tee shot on the fifth, and a perfectly stroked seven iron to 10 feet earned the first birdie. A six iron to 20 feet on the sixth and a curling putt that

fell earned the second; and then Nick reached the green of the seventh with two big downwind shots, a drive and a three iron to 40 feet. He took two putts and had his third.

Four under par now and closing in. A drive and three iron to 25 feet on the eighth followed by a two iron and nine iron set up two pars. Faldo had played the first nine in 31, equalling Henry Cotton's record set in 1934 and matched by Senior in the first round. Faldo wasn't through yet.

Hitting one precise shot after another, Nick set up another birdie opportunity by laying a nine iron 12 feet from the hole on the 10th green, but he missed the putt. A chance gone. A five iron to 20 feet and two putts earned his par on the 11th; a wedge to six feet on the 12th and Faldo was looking at another birdie. Once again, though, his putter failed him and he settled for still another par.

Still four under par for the round, he stood one

Yoshinori Mizumaki had 31 on the second nine.

Ernie Els (137) said his 1992 experience was a benefit.

stroke behind Couples, two behind Langer. He was on his way to 66 if he could hold his game together as the wind criss-crossed the fairways, forcing him to work the ball back and forth according to the wind's direction.

Now, though, Faldo made another move. A three wood from the tee followed by another great iron, a nine iron to four feet, and another holed putt. Five under par for the round. Now he had caught Couples with the 14th, the Suez Canal, a definite birdie hole, coming up. One more birdie and he would climb level with Langer and share the 36-hole lead.

A loose drive here almost cost him a stroke. His ball veered left and dived into the knee-high rough, safe from the out of bounds flanking the right side, but still in trouble. From there Nick tried to slash it out with a five iron, but the club turned in his hand. He cleared the Suez, but his ball settled back in the rough. From there he dug it out with a seven iron that squirted across the fairway into the light rough on the opposite side, still about 50 yards short of the green. Three shots played and still not on.

Now Faldo played one of those shots that win championships. He hit a nice pitch that braked, trickled slowly toward the hole, hit the flagstick gently, and tumbled into the cup. A birdie 4 where a par looked the best he could do. Now he stood six under par for the round, seven under for the 32 holes, and he had caught Langer. He wasn't through yet; he still had four hard holes to play.

Safely past the 15th with a drive and another precise five iron inside 20 feet, another five iron to 15 feet on the 16th, and a drive and four iron to 25 feet on the difficult 17th. Three pars, but not out of danger yet.

As Faldo strode on to the tee of the 18th he felt the fresh wind blowing directly into his face, turning the home hole into a severe test. Nick nailed as good a drive as he had hit throughout the afternoon and followed with another perfectly struck shot, a terrific two iron that bored through the wind, skipped on to the green, and pulled up just 12 feet from the cup. The putt fell, Faldo had come home in 32, shot 63 for the round, and passed Langer. He had taken command of the Open.

Barry Lane (138) missed two greens in 36 holes.

This was as good a round as anyone had ever played in an Open, filled with stirring shots that split the fairways and covered the flagsticks. It followed the pattern he had set a year earlier at Muirfield, where he shot 64 in the second round and took command of the championship. Whether it would work the same effect here wouldn't be determined for two more days, but it indeed vaulted Faldo to the front and put him into the record book, for he had broken the course record set by Christy O'Connor, Jr, in the 1985 Open, and become one of six men who had shot 63 in an Open — Mark Hayes at Turnberry in 1977, Isao Aoki at Muirfield in 1980, Greg Norman at Turnberry in 1986, Paul Broadhurst at St Andrews in 1990 and Jodie Mudd at Royal Birkdale in 1991.

In with 132 for 36 holes, Faldo still couldn't feel too comfortable, for aside from Langer and Couples, Norman had suddenly sprung to life. Playing immediately behind Faldo, Norman, who had opened with 66, had gone out in 34 with two birdies and a bogey on the tough fifth, but he picked up birdies on both the 12th and 13th and missed a chance for a third at the 14th. Two crisp shots left him just short of the green, but his chip ran well past the hole. He settled for a par on a hole where he should have counted on a birdie.

Sandy Lyle (146), the 1985 champion here, was out by three strokes after 76 in the second round.

Greg saved par on the 15th after overshooting the green with a five-iron second, then dropped another stroke at the hard 17th, where he drove into the rough. Back in 34, he shot 68 and fell from a tie for first into a tie for third, at 134, with Couples and Pavin, who shot 66 with six birdies and two bogeys, one on that demanding 11th.

Meantime, Senior, one of the four co-leaders, dropped to sixth place, at 135, and Zoeller fell into a

Ian Baker-Finch (142) qualified by one stroke.

tie for seventh with Mize, at 136.

This was a magnificent leaderboard; six of those first eight players had won one or more of the four most important tournaments in the game. Only Senior and Pavin hadn't. Four were among the Sony Ranking's top-five golfers in the world. It all confirmed that Royal St George's ranks among the world's great examinations in the game.

Full of wonderful golf, the day, at the same time, had been cruel, for so many of the game's great figures had been eliminated. The 36-hole cut fell at 143, just three strokes over par. Among those who would play no further, the crowds mourned the loss of Jack Nicklaus, Gary Player, Tony Jacklin and Tom Watson, who had given the galleries so many exciting moments in the past; Ben Crenshaw, everybody's favourite; Sandy Lyle, who had won at this same place in 1985; Davis Love III, who had never done well in the most important competitions; Jose Maria Olazabal; and two men who had figured so prominently in the 1992 championship — John Cook, whose missed two-foot birdie putt on the 17th at Muirfield and his bogey on the 18th opened the way for Faldo to win, and Steve Pate, who had put early pressure on Nick in the last round.

Some of them had been close to qualifying. Nicklaus slipped five over par on the last seven holes and missed by one stroke. Watson worked his way back to three over with a birdie on the 16th, but then bogeyed the 17th and missed by one stroke as well.

Gary Player (144) exited by one stroke.

Tom Watson (144) also did not qualify.

Nick Faldo was pointing to a fourth Open title.

SECOND ROUND RESULTS

HOLE	1	2	3	4	5	6	7	8	9	10	11	12	13	14	15	16	17	18	
PAR	4	4	3	4	4	3	5	4	4	4	3	4	4	5	4	3	4	4	TOTAL
Nick Faldo	3	4	3	4	3	2	4	4	4	4	3	4	3	4	4	3	4	3	63-132
Bernhard Langer	3	4	3	4	4	3	4	3	4	4	2	4	4	4	4	3	4	5	66-133
Fred Couples	4	3	2	4	4	3	4	5	3	4	3	3	3	4	4	3	5	5	66-134
Greg Norman	4	3	3	4	5	2	5	4	4	4	3	3	3	5	4	3	5	4	68-134
Corey Pavin	4	4	4	4	4	2	4	4	3	4	3	3	3	5	3	3	5	4	66-134
Peter Senior	4	4	2	5	4	3	4	4	4	3	3	4	3	5	5	3	5	4	69-135
Fuzzy Zoeller	4	4	3	4	4	3	5	5	3	4	3	4	3	5	4	3	5	4	70-136
Larry Mize	3	4	4	4	4	2	4	4	4	4	3	4	4	4	4	3	5	5	69-136
Peter Baker	4	4	3	4	3	2	5	4	4	5	3	4	4	5	4	2	3	4	67-137
Ernie Els	4	3	4	4	5	2	4	4	4	4	3	3	4	6	5	3	3	4	69-137
John Daly	4	3	3	4	4	2	4	3	4	4	3	3	4	4	4	3	6	4	66-137

HOLE SUMMARY

HOLE	PAR	EAGLES	BIRDIES	PARS	BOGEYS	HIGHER	RANK	AVERAGE
1	4	0	23	108	25	0	14	4.01
2	4	0	25	117	12	2	16	3.94
3	3	0	8	93	50	5	3	3.33
4	4	0	4	84	55	13	1	4.51
5	4	0	13	114	28	1	10	4.11
6	3	0	33	102	19	2	17	2.94
7	5	13	86	50	7	0	18	4.33
8	4	0	10	87	54	5	6	4.35
9	4	0	18	108	24	6	9	4.13
OUT	35	13	220	863	274	34		35.65
10	4	0	12	94	41	9	7	4.32
11	3	0	7	95	49	5	3	3.33
12	4	0	26	101	27	2	13	4.03
13	4	1	32	91	31	1	15	3.99
14	5	0	32	91	22	11	12	5.09
15	4	0	17	92	42	5	8	4.22
16	3	0	19	110	26	1	11	3.06
17	4	0	9	84	53	10	5	4.41
18	4	0	4	82	60	10	2	4.49
IN	35	1	158	840	351	54		36.94
TOTAL	70	14	378	1703	625	88		72.59

Players Below Par	26
Players At Par	16
Players Above Par	114

LOW SCORES

Low First Nine	John Daly	31
	Nick Faldo	31
Low Second Nine	Yoshinori Mizumaki	31
Low Round	Nick Faldo	63

The Golf Exhibition was busy with many shoppers — and autograph seekers.

3

PAVIN CLIMBS AS SCORES FALL

BY ROBERT SOMMERS

From a total of 312 rounds during the first 36 holes, the field of the 122nd Open Championship had played 73 rounds in the 60s, which breaks down to 23 percent, a little less than one quarter of the rounds over perhaps the most difficult course in the Open rota. It appears obvious, then, that given the proper conditions, the modern professional golfer might shoot anything; he has not approached his limit.

Even the most common defences don't guarantee to frustrate players at this level. Distance means nothing. Accustomed to courses that reach beyond 7,000 yards, the 6,860 yards of Royal St George's stood well within their range. Heavy rough, speedy greens and tough hole locations have more effect. Sandwich had all the rough even a sadist might wish for, and whilst green speed may have lagged behind some the players find in other championships, the positions of the holes caught everyone's attention.

As the third round began, the early players found the flagsticks set next to hollows, bumps and ridges. A number of putts broke twice. Nevertheless, not long into the day the course still showed it could be beaten. Starting off around 10 o'clock, Tom Kite, returning to the site of an earlier disappointment, and Ian Baker-Finch were the first to turn in sub-par scores.

Kite had been leading the 1985 Open with nine holes to play, but he missed the 10th green, dumped his third shot into a bunker, bladed his fourth across

Wayne Grady was out in 30 for his 64-206.

the green, and made 6. Surely and steadily he fell from the chase. A year ago, though, he had won the 1992 US Open, at Pebble Beach, but injuries had bothered him ever since.

After opening with 72 on Thursday and following with 70 on Friday, Kite sped around Royal St George's in 68 in the third round, a boost to his morale but of no real consequence to the final result of the championship.

Tom hadn't been finished 10 minutes before Baker-Finch followed him in with a round of 67. Clearly, even though the greens had dried out somewhat and the holes had been set in baffling positions, the course would yield to first-class shot-making.

The strongest signal that Royal St George's might be in for another rough day came from Wayne Grady, the 1990 USPGA champion. Playing immediately behind Baker-Finch, Grady shot 64, and had finished before the eight leaders had begun.

To refresh memories, Grady had led the 1989 Open going into the last round with scores of 68, 67 and 69, but he slipped to 71 in the fourth round, Greg Norman roared around Royal Troon in 64, and Mark Calcavecchia finished with 68. Both men had caught him. Calcavecchia, of course, won the play-off. Disappointed, Grady made up for it by winning the USPGA the following August.

He hadn't done much since then, and in fact hadn't won a tournament on the American tour. He had, in fact, missed the cut in seven of the 13 events he had

AN OPEN LOST IN A BUSH

BY MARINO PARASCENZO

Arnold Palmer has a plaque at Royal Birkdale. Ben Hogan has a bridge at Augusta. Golf has a lot of monuments. There's even one at Royal St George's to Bernhard Langer, from the 1993 Open Championship. But it's not the same kind of thing at all.

Langer's monument marks the occasion of his not winning the Open again. In fact, this monument was the principle reason that he didn't. It wasn't erected after the fact, it was already there, just waiting for him. As monuments go, it's not much.

But it didn't have to be much. Just a small hawthorn bush. Langer, looking for his second major title of the year and the third of his career — he had won his second US Masters in April — was right up there among the leaders, eight under par and tied with Nick Faldo and Corey Pavin in the third round. And then he hit his approach shot at the eighth hole, and it somehow ended up in that little bush. In due time, he walked off with a double-bogey 6. There went another Open.

It might be argued that Langer also had a double bogey at the 14th in the final round, and that hurt just as badly. Of course it did. The point is, anyone can hit a tee shot out of bounds. But how many hit that bush?

Langer probably leads the present-day players in 'almosts' at the Open. In 15 Opens, this was his fifth 'almost' — a second, a tie for second, a third (this

Langer kicked in a 20-foot birdie.

time) and two ties for third. Ironically, three of his 'almosts' came at Royal St George's: a second behind Bill Rogers in 1981, a tie for third behind Sandy Lyle in 1985 and a third behind Greg Norman this time.

Langer is as tough and springy as that hawthorn bush and hungrier than almost everyone, and he's also one of the most graceful in the face of failure and frustration. He missed the six-foot putt at the final hole that cost Europe the 1991 Ryder Cup match. He broke down and cried, but he came back the next week and won the German Masters.

And so at Royal St George's, as Norman wrapped up his second Open title in the final round, Langer could only shrug. He was playing alongside Norman and watching his own chances drain away, stroke by stroke. Langer was shooting 67, after all. With rounds of 67, 66, 70 and 67, Langer finished three strokes behind Norman and with the knowledge that his 10-under-par 270 total would have won all but two Opens.

'Well, it's disappointing because it's the one championship I would like to win more than any other one,' Langer said. 'But I'm not too disappointed because I played quite well. At the beginning of the day, someone might have thought a 67, 10 under, might win the tournament. But as it turned out, Greg had an unbelievable day. He played some of the best golf I've ever seen anywhere. And under the circumstances — the last round of a major championship

Langer has won two US Masters titles, but has been frustrated in his attempts for the Open Championship.

on a tough golf course — it's just incredible.'

Langer never once mentioned the hawthorn bush. 'Was that a bad bounce?' someone asked. 'A very unlucky bounce,' said Langer calmly. 'That bush is 10 yards short and 15 yards wide, and there's nothing else around for 50 yards.'

The eighth hole is a 418-yard par 4, a slight dogleg to the right from where the fairway crests and starts gently downhill. The shot from there is a four iron or five iron. You don't even notice the hawthorn bush, near the gallery rope far to the right. It's perched on a rise about four feet above the fairway, and sits about even with the front of the green, strangely alone. The bush is dome-shaped, only about three feet high at its rounded peak, and about six feet in diameter, an angry snarl of branches covered with ripping thorns.

The fourth-hardest hole of the Open, the eighth averaged a quarter-stroke over par. Langer nearly birdied it in the first round, knocking a four iron to eight feet and just missing the putt. He nearly eagled it in the second round, firing a three iron to a mere three inches. In the third round, after he birdied the seventh to catch Faldo and Pavin at eight under par, he ended up in the bush.

Langer looked at it for a moment, then gingerly reached in and lifted the ball out.

There were 11 double bogeys at No. 8 during the championship, but only one by a contender. Aside from being baffled, Langer had little to say. Of course, the double bogey at the 14th in the final round also hurt him, but he dismissed it with a clinical description. 'Very simple,' he said. 'Driver out of bounds, one iron off the tee, another three iron, nine iron and two putts.'

And third place. Victory denied again. How was this one compared to the other three? Langer stood by the fence outside the scoring trailer, just a few yards from the 18th green, and rummaged through the memories of Opens missed.

'Actually, they were all a little different,' Langer said. 'In 1984, when I tied for second at St Andrews — when Seve won and I was tied with Watson — I played very well from tee to green, but I couldn't make any putts. This week, I made numerous putts, and I just made a few bad shots here and there, and someone else played better.

'In 1985, when I was here, on this course, with a chance to win going into the last day, I shot 75 and was very disappointed, because if I shot 72, I think I would have won the tournament. I remember missing a short putt on the first, and getting a lot of bad breaks, bad bounces out there, which can easily happen. And one shot slid away after another. So they were all a little different.'

In the late 1970s and early 1980s, Langer was fast becoming a force in European golf. He tied for 51st in his second Open, in 1980 at Muirfield, then rocketed to prominence at Royal St George's in 1981. That was Bill Rogers' year. He seemed to win, somewhere, every fifth time he teed it up, and one of those was the Open at Royal St George's. It was easy to forget who finished second.

In the third round, Langer eagled the 14th with a 50-foot putt to get within two strokes of Rogers, but bogeyed the 17th with an approach shot through the green. In the fourth round, he held his game together with his putting. He birdied the seventh from 10 feet, then saved par at the eighth to close within one stroke.

'Bernhard was sitting there, not making any mistakes,' Rogers was to say later. But the mistakes — or misfortunes — came. Langer hit into a bunker at the 11th and his golf ball was caught under the lip. At the 15th, he took two strokes to get out of another bunker. At the 17th, he missed a three-foot putt for par.

He was second by four strokes, but the performance got him an invitation to his first US Masters, in 1982. He won his first US Masters title in 1985, in his second appearance, which in turn had followed his second close call in the Open, in 1984 at St Andrews. He had spent the week preceding the Open in bed with influenza, and then he proceeded to waltz around the Old Course without hitting into a bunker until the third round, that at the 14th, which cost him his lone bogey of the day. He had already made three birdies in succession, on a 15-foot putt at the fourth, then a lip-out from 90 feet and a tap-in at the fifth and an 18-footer at the sixth. He also birdied the 15th and 16th, then saved par from the Road Bunker at the 17th. If ever an Open was his, this was it. For a while.

Starting the 1984 Open, Langer had said Watson was the man to beat. It would have been three Open victories in a row for Watson. Ballesteros, on the other hand, had said that Langer was the man to beat. No one had asked about Ian Baker-Finch, but it was his Open until he bogeyed No. 1 in the final

Langer has an unusual, but successful putting style.

round. He faded rapidly from there. Langer caught everyone's eye when he nearly holed out his approach shot at the first for an eagle. The birdie got him to within one stroke of Watson, then trouble set in.

Langer bogeyed the third from a bunker, and bogeyed the fifth with three putts. He was wonderful coming down the stretch. He two-putted the 16th from 60 feet for a par, saved par at the 17th again with two putts from 70 feet, then birdied from above the hole at the 18th. He had been upstaged, though, with Watson losing the lead with a bad approach at the 17th, and Ballesteros, just ahead, making a brilliant par at the 17th and then a brilliant birdie at the 18th. Watson and Langer tied for second place, two strokes behind, at 10-under-par 278.

Corey Pavin (68-202) acknowledged the applause as he joined Nick Faldo in the lead after 54 holes.

'That bush is 10 yards short and 15 yards wide,' said Bernhard Langer, 'and there's nothing else around for 50 yards.'

Greg Norman (69-203) again drove well.

entered in 1993, and had won very little money, less than US$40,000, and had fallen to 172nd place in the rankings of US money winners. Consequently, nothing much had been expected of him at Sandwich, especially after he began with 74 on Thursday, a score that clearly placed him in danger of missing the 36-hole cut. Pulling his game together, he rallied by shooting 68 in the second round and saved himself.

Still, he represented no threat just yet. At 142 he stood well behind the leaders, trailing Nick Faldo by 10 strokes, but he continued to fight and began his third round with two birdies, reaching the right rear of the first green with an eight iron and holing from six feet and following with a sand wedge to another pin position close to the ridge edge and rolling home the putt from 10 feet.

Grady had his biggest moment on the seventh. After a solid drive, Wayne ripped into a three wood that rolled on to the green about 25 feet from the hole, tucked only four paces from the left edge. Grady's putt tumbled into the hole. An eagle 3; two strokes gained on one hole.

Now he stood four under par for the round, but still a long way from the lead. Determined, he continued to plug away and played a stunning six iron into the eighth that braked just 10 feet from the hole. Another putt fell and another 3 went down on his scorecard, his sixth of the round. He was five under through eight holes. When he played a routine par 4 at the ninth, he had gone out in 30, the best nine-hole score of the championship. Anything seemed possible now.

Grady began the homeward half still playing remarkable golf. He threaded a nine iron on to the elevated 10th green within five feet of the cup, set dangerously close to the right side, where the ground falls away down a slight slope. The putt dropped and he picked up still another 3. A par at the 11th and he had his eighth 3 and only three 4s. He was playing stunning golf.

Now he stood six under par with seven holes left. He had been playing such precise irons and had putted so well, holing every makeable putt, that his gallery had the feeling he might shoot anything.

Now the wind grew stronger, still coming in from the southwest, as it had throughout the week. Grady made par figures through the next six holes, and then stepped on to the 18th tee feeling the full force of the wind coming directly at him. He lashed into his driver and drilled his ball within 240 yards of the green. Not sure he could make the green from that distance, he drew out his driver once again. He was right; he couldn't make it. His ball pulled up about 40 yards short of the green, but a nice pitch to 10 feet saved the par. He had come back in 34, and his 64 raised him to the fringes of the contenders, at 206 for 54 holes, within reach of the leaders. He had played a remarkable round made up of nine 3s, eight 4s and one 5, a par on the 14th. Sensational as it had been, Grady's round could have been even better; putts grazed the lips of the holes on the 16th and 17th, but didn't fall.

Bernhard Langer (70-203) was unhappy with his woods.

Norman went to eight under par with this 30-foot birdie at the 11th, but then he made bogey at the 15th.

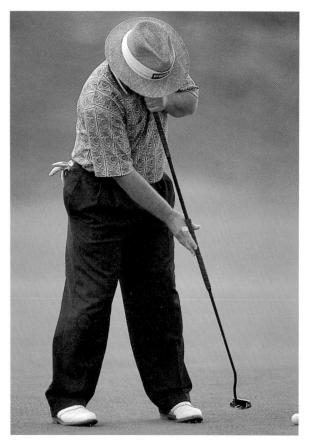

Peter Senior (205) had a 30-foot eagle at the seventh.

Ernie Els (206) dropped two shots on the second nine.

Nick Price, discussing strategy with caddie Jeff (Squeaky) Medlen, shot 67-205 to be joint fifth.

Pavin rolled in a 30-foot birdie at the 16th to tie for the lead at eight under par.

As Grady worked his way among the leaders, two others made significant moves as well. While Grady played those last treacherous holes, Nick Price set out on his way to a round of 67 that put him solidly into the chase at 205, but the big move was made by Corey Pavin, a pint-sized American with an unorthodox swing and a deadly putting stroke.

Starting out two strokes behind Faldo, at 134 for 36 holes, Pavin shot 68. When Faldo came in later with an even-par round of 70, Pavin had tied him for first place, at 202, one stroke ahead of Bernhard Langer, who matched Faldo's 70, and Greg Norman, who shot 69. With 70, Peter Senior dropped to a tie for fifth place, with Price, while Fred Couples shot 72, a round that would cost him heavily. He dropped into a tie with Grady and the young South African Ernie Els.

At first glance, Pavin gives the impression he has no business competing against the best players in the game. He lists his height at 5-ft-9, but he's probably an inch or so shorter, and his weight at 10 stone, which might be overstating it. Nevertheless, he had performed well enough in both his amateur and professional careers to have won places on both the Walker Cup and Ryder Cup teams and won every one of his singles matches.

Nor is he prone to intimidation. During his professional career he has won 10 tournaments, five of them in play-offs. He's lost only two.

The other US players consider him the most reliable clutch putter in the game, and he has holed some remarkable shots in spite of a jerky-looking swing that finishes with his hands low and almost wrapped around his left shoulder. His most gritty moment may have come at the end of the 1992 Honda Classic, in Florida, where he holed a full eight-iron shot to tie Couples, then won the play-off by holing a 20-foot putt.

A month later he placed third in the US Masters, helped considerably by a hole-in-one on Augusta National's hazardous 16th.

Not a big man himself, Langer speaks highly of Pavin's ability, saying, 'He's a tremendous competitor for his size. If I had to put anybody on the line to make a putt for me, I would choose him every time.'

Price called Pavin one of the smartest players in the game, saying, 'He was not given a lot to play this game with. He's not as long a hitter as I am, nor

Nick Faldo (70-202) hit his approach shot at the 17th, his 13th of 14 successive pars.

Norman nor Couples, but he's a fierce competitor.'

Nor is Pavin, like most Americans, unfamiliar with links golf. He played the European Tour for three and a half months during 1983, shortly after he became a professional and before he qualified for the American tour. During that period he won twice and placed 13th on the Order of Merit. Once he qualified for the American tour, he became the first player since Jack Nicklaus to win a tournament in each of his first five years. Seven years after joining the tour, he became the 1991 leading money winner.

Fully confident in his ability to compete at the game's highest levels, Pavin, who was paired with Senior, made his move early, playing a nice little pitch to 10 feet on the second for one birdie. Then, barely on the fourth green following a drive and a four wood, he holed another putt that must have covered 50 feet.

Eight under par now, he had caught Faldo, who was off to a shaky start. With Prince Andrew, a certifiable golf nut, in his gallery, Nick bore up under

an uncomfortable moment on the first tee. Just as he reached the top of that fluid backswing, a spectator, obviously intending to distract him, unleashed a piercing whistle. Nick flinched coming into the ball and hit the shot a bit thin, although it flew straight enough. His features set in a grim expression, Nick marched down the fairway while the Prince snapped, 'That was appalling.'

The culprit was chased down and expelled from the course.

Nick, meantime, had matched Pavin's birdie on the second with an even better approach, laying a wedge inside seven feet, taking over the lead once again at nine under par, but the course struck back, taking a stroke away from him on that hard fourth hole, where the drive must clear a high mound pitted with what must be the game's largest bunker.

Faldo avoided the bunker, but his ball landed in the high rough, leaving him no option other than a safe seven iron and a wedge to 20 feet. With the bogey, Faldo fell back to eight under par, even with

Pavin once again, and with Langer, who was paired with him.

Now Norman was closing in as well. Driving as well as he ever had (he didn't miss a fairway all day), he laced a six iron to 10 feet on the first, dropping him to seven under par and within one stroke of the lead, but he missed a great chance for another on the seventh. Perhaps the longest straight driver in the game, Norman drilled another long tee shot that brought the green of this 530-yard par 5 within six-iron range. His ball stopped about 25 feet from the hole, but Greg three-putted, losing a chance to pull even with Faldo and Pavin.

While Norman was giving away an opportunity,

Couples, who was paired with him, struggled with an inconsistent game. A bogey on the fourth, where his approach rolled down the slope to the right of the green, dropped him to five under, and then he drove into a fairway bunker on the seventh. His ball lodged among the layers of sod, giving him very little chance to play a reasonable second. From there he advanced the ball only about 30 yards, his third shot ran to the back of the green about 40 feet past the hole, and he too needed three putts. Another bogey, and Couples fell further back, now only four under par for 43 holes.

As Norman and Couples struggled, cheers from behind them led their gallery to believe Faldo was

Fred Couples (72-206) struggled with four bogeys and two birdies.

Gil Morgan (70-208).

John Daly (70-207).

Raymond Floyd had 31 on second nine.

doing great things, but it turned out the cheering had been for a save by Langer on the fourth hole, where he drove into the rough and needed two more shots to reach the green before holing from 12 feet.

A big drive on the seventh and a four iron to 18 feet set up a two-putt birdie, and when Faldo couldn't answer, instead pushing his second shot into a bunker and struggling to hole a three-foot putt to save a par, Langer slipped into a tie for the lead at eight under par with Faldo and Pavin.

As quickly as he tied for the lead, though, Langer dropped behind. His drive on the eighth drifted into the right rough, and he followed with an inexcusable shot, a four iron pushed far right. His ball skimmed along the line of spectators held back by ropes that cordon off the fairways, barely missed a woman leaning over to watch him, flew behind the head of an observer seated on a shooting stick inside the ropes, and disappeared into a lonely, full-bodied hawthorn bush sitting on a hillside at least 15 yards short of the green, and perhaps 15 yards to the right. It was a terrible shot, and Langer was lucky to find his ball.

But he did. It was clearly unplayable, and it cost him a double-bogey 6. He was two strokes behind Faldo and Pavin now.

Up ahead, Pavin had gone out in 33 and started back by saving a par on the 10th with deft work around the green, chipping to four feet after missing

with a five-iron approach, and holing the putt. He stood eight under par, still even with Faldo.

Corey continued to play error-free golf until he reached the 15th. He drove well, leaving himself 162 yards short of the green, but from there he evidently under-clubbed. Three bunkers cross the fairways like pearls in a necklace a few yards short of the green. When his ball caught the top of the bunker's face, killing its forward momentum, Pavin cried, 'Oh, no.'

His ball pulled up a good 10 feet short, and he bogeyed, dropping a stroke behind Faldo and Norman, who by then had birdied the 11th with a long, 30-foot putt.

Pavin is a fighter, though; he doesn't give up easily. Realizing he needed a birdie, he rifled a five iron to the 16th about 30 feet from the cup. As confident a putter as ever lived, Corey stroked his ball into the cup. Back to eight under par, tied with Faldo.

Just as Pavin was birdieing the 16th, Norman, immediately behind him, missed the 15th green to the right, putted up the slope, and bogeyed, dropping back to seven under. Routine pars on both the 16th and 17th brought him to that trying finishing hole. There he hit a screaming drive that seemed would never come down. When it did, Norman had nothing but a five iron left on a hole where Grady couldn't reach the green with two drivers. Greg's approach rolled off the back of the green, but a chip to five feet and a nerveless putt earned him his par.

That is how Norman finished, shooting 69, tying Langer, who shot 70, at 203, one stroke behind Faldo and Pavin, the co-leaders at 202, eight under par.

As machine-like as ever, Faldo had ground out 14 consecutive pars after his bogey on the fourth, and he struggled for only three of those — on the sixth, where he holed from six feet after mis-hitting his tee shot; on the seventh, and on the 16th, where he ran in another six-footer.

Playing much better than anyone could have anticipated, Senior shot 70 and matched Price at 205, and Seve Ballesteros shot 69, not low enough to make him a threat but plenty good enough to delight his fans.

Jose Rivero (67-208) advanced to joint 12th place.

Langer and Faldo wave to the crowd surrounding the 18th green.

THIRD ROUND RESULTS

HOLE	1	2	3	4	5	6	7	8	9	10	11	12	13	14	15	16	17	18	
PAR	4	4	3	4	4	3	5	4	4	4	3	4	4	5	4	3	4	4	TOTAL
Corey Pavin	4	3	3	3	4	3	5	4	4	4	3	4	4	5	5	2	4	4	68-202
Nick Faldo	4	3	3	5	4	3	5	4	4	4	3	4	4	5	4	3	4	4	70-202
Greg Norman	3	4	3	4	4	3	5	4	4	4	2	4	4	5	5	3	4	4	69-203
Bernhard Langer	4	3	3	4	4	4	4	6	4	4	3	4	4	5	4	2	4	4	70-203
Nick Price	3	3	3	4	4	3	4	4	4	5	3	3	3	5	4	4	4	4	67-205
Peter Senior	4	4	3	5	4	3	4	4	4	3	4	3	5	5	4	3	4	4	70-205
Wayne Grady	3	3	3	4	4	3	3	3	4	3	3	4	4	5	4	3	4	4	64-206
Ernie Els	3	3	3	4	3	3	5	3	4	3	4	4	5	5	3	4	5		69-206
Fred Couples	4	4	3	5	4	3	6	5	4	3	3	4	4	5	4	2	5	4	72-206
John Daly	4	3	3	4	4	3	5	5	4	4	3	4	4	4	4	4	4	4	70-207
Fuzzy Zoeller	4	4	3	5	4	3	4	5	4	4	4	3	5	4	4	3	5	3	71-207
Jose Rivero	4	4	2	4	4	4	5	4	4	4	3	3	4	5	4	2	3	4	67-208
Gil Morgan	4	4	3	4	3	3	4	5	4	4	3	3	5	5	5	3	4	4	70-208

HOLE SUMMARY

HOLE	PAR	EAGLES	BIRDIES	PARS	BOGEYS	HIGHER	RANK	AVERAGE
1	4	0	12	54	11	1	12	4.01
2	4	0	23	49	5	1	17	3.79
3	3	0	4	53	19	2	2	3.24
4	4	0	5	49	22	2	4	4.27
5	4	0	5	56	16	1	7	4.17
6	3	0	10	52	16	0	11	3.08
7	5	5	38	32	3	0	18	4.42
8	4	0	5	48	23	2	3	4.28
9	4	0	5	50	21	2	5	4.26
OUT	35	5	107	443	136	11		35.52
10	4	0	13	51	14	0	12	4.01
11	3	0	9	53	16	0	10	3.09
12	4	0	11	58	9	0	14	3.97
13	4	0	10	51	14	3	9	4.13
14	5	0	19	53	5	1	16	4.85
15	4	0	4	54	20	0	6	4.21
16	3	0	14	55	9	0	15	2.94
17	4	0	5	57	10	0	8	4.14
18	4	0	2	47	26	3	1	4.38
IN	35	0	87	479	129	7		35.72
TOTAL	70	5	194	922	265	18		71.24

			LOW SCORES	
Players Below Par	16	Low First Nine	Wayne Grady	30
Players At Par	13	Low Second Nine	Raymond Floyd	31
Players Above Par	49	Low Round	Wayne Grady	64

Refreshments at Royal St George's were available in many forms.

Nick Faldo was the hot favourite to win the Open Championship again.

THE MAN TO BEAT

BY ALISTER NICOL

Reigning Open champion Nick Faldo slept well on the night of Saturday 17 July, the eve of his 36th birthday. And with good reason. Not only was he rated No. 1 on the Sony Ranking, but he had also been installed by Britain's bookmakers as the hot favourite to win his third Open title in seven years. When Faldo closed his eyes in Sandwich that Saturday night, he did so in the satisfying knowledge that he shared the lead at eight under par after 54 holes with American Corey Pavin following rounds of 69, a record-equalling 63 and a par 70.

No one knows what thoughts he had before drifting off to sleep but, vastly experienced competitor that he is, Nick must have been reasonably confident that a sub-par round Sunday would be good enough for him to repeat his 1992 win at Muirfield. Surely his mind must also have gone back to Muirfield in 1987. That was the year he claimed his first Open title with 18 par figures on the Sunday to defeat Paul Azinger.

Few players can 'read' situations as well as Faldo, the man who has raised clinical dedication to an art form, with three Open and two US Masters victories in a torrid six-year spell of domination of world golf. To be sharing the lead with Pavin, scarcely a name to strike fear and trembling into hearts, and be one ahead of Greg Norman and Bernhard Langer must have been a comforting thought.

Major championships carry unique pressures. Having to play catch-up on such an intimidating figure as Faldo in his prime is sure to have weighed as heavily as a deep-sea diver's boots on the chasing pack. It

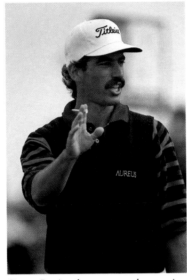

Corey Pavin also was ready to win.

was going to take an exceptional round of golf to halt Faldo, who was not only in the mood but in seemingly invincible mode.

Co-leader Pavin had built his reputation as a fierce competitor, a man respected and admired by his peers for playing within his own capabilities and one able to manoeuvre the ball in the fashion links golf frequently demands. Could he be the man to match the 63 with which his Sunday partner had ignited Royal St George's on the Friday?

Pavin had fired a third-round 68 when the pin placements were the toughest of the week and declared, 'I am always ready to win my first major, but I fear I will not be ready too much longer. Right now all the cards are in place, and I am playing very well. There is no weakness in my game, and while I do not like to lose, it will not be the end of the world if I don't win.

'I want to win a major and if I go through my career without one, it will be disappointing, but I will not let my career ride on a major title. Faldo is the best player in the world right now, one who is not going to make too many mistakes tomorrow. He has done it all before and he will be tough. But I can be tough.'

Only one behind were those formidable foreigners, Norman from Australia and Germany's tungsten-tough Langer, who had marched away from the field at Augusta in April to earn his second US Masters green jacket.

There can be scarcely a handful of golfers in the game with as much going for them as the outrageously gifted Norman, but Faldo would have been comforted by the memory of withstanding Norman's

The pursuit of an Open Championship can be a lonely trail.

last-round 63 in the Johnnie Walker World Championship in Jamaica just before Christmas in 1992, then beating him in a play-off. Provided Faldo could beat par, he must have felt, justifiably, that he would remain in the driver's seat.

Yet Norman, for whom the world had waited years to fulfil his potential, had the confidence which matters so much in the stratosphere of super-stardom. After his 68 in the second round, he was two behind the defending champion and refused to be overawed by Nick's 63.

'I know I have at least one 63 in me,' he said, without even a suggestion of bravado, 'and Nick Faldo is not infallible.' Twenty-four hours later, little had happened to make the Great White Shark change his mind. In fact, as he slipped into joint second with a round to go, he proclaimed that Faldo was not the principal threat.

Was he attempting to pressurize the champion? Was he merely deleting negative bytes from his own mental computer? Was he even the teeniest bit fearful of the defending champion shooting his third sub-70 round of the 122nd Open Championship and leaving Greg with the 1986 Open title his only major?

Langer has always been a man unto himself, sure of his own mind and the direction he wants to travel down life's highways and by-ways. The bricklayer's son from Bavaria has always done things his way, even to the extent of declaring in his early teens that he wanted to be a professional golfer. He was laughed out of class by his teachers, who scoffed at the idea of any German youngster wanting to make a career in a silly game like golf. He was undaunted by their derision, and has remained fearless of most things in life ever since.

A winner every year since he made the breakthrough in 1980, Langer's ultimate goal has been to win the Open. It means more to him than any other championship in golf, and he has been infuriatingly close. In 1985 at Royal St George's, his chip to tie Sandy Lyle actually hit the hole and spun out.

The previous year at St Andrews, he had played alongside Seve Ballesteros on the last day only to shoot 71 to the inspired Spaniard's 69 on the Old Course and finished in a tie for second with Tom Watson. Back then, the German did not know the Spaniard very well and later admitted he had found Seve 'intimidating.' Langer had become totally bewildered by Seve's near-total silence during the entire tension-packed round.

For a long time he even suspected Seve of unsportsmanlike behaviour, until he appreciated that was simply the way Seve went about getting the job done.

Langer learned from that experience and is now a fearsomely dedicated competitor in his own right. In common with his peers, he has tremendous respect and admiration for what Faldo has done in golf. He and Nick share unbounded dedication in the search for what they perceive as perfection.

Langer, who is allergic to trees and grass, incidentally, had adhered strictly to a pre-tournament game plan to put himself in the position of only one behind going into the crunch final round at Royal St George's. Pivotal to that plan was a determination to hit nothing more than a one iron from the tee at the dangerous par-5 14th, with the out-of-bounds Prince's course lying in wait for a slightly errant tee shot to the right. Langer decided from the start that the hole had to be played strictly as a par 5, with any one-putt birdie a welcome bonus.

Like Norman, Langer refused to concede that Faldo was the only threat to his title hopes. He said after a third-round 70, 'There are a lot of good players out there, and anyone within four or five shots has a chance. Pavin and Norman are right in there, and they have won many tournaments between them.

'Pavin may not be as long as Norman and other players, but he has imagination, he can draw or fade the ball and his short game is brilliant. That is important here.'

He refused to be drawn about his own chances, but obviously felt very good about them, knowing that the neck problems which had hampered his normally meticulous preparation has eased significantly. Privately he fancied his chances. Another round in the 60s to set beside his opening 67 and 66, and the old claret jug might finally be his, and a dream fulfilled.

Two shots behind Bernhard and Greg lay the menace of Nick Price, current USPGA champion and enjoying a year of unprecedented success in America, with more than US$1 million in official earnings and three victories so far. Indeed, when he arrived at

Sandwich the 'Other Nick' had racked up an unrivalled seven worldwide wins since the previous August including the USPGA. The credentials of the man who had twice come close to taking golf's oldest and most prestigious prize — at Royal Troon in 1983 and Royal Lytham five years later — were impeccable. He was one of 'four or five' to whom Langer had referred.

We do not know whether Australian Peter Senior came into Langer's reckoning. At 5-ft-5 and 13 stone, the 34-year-old from Brisbane and a European Tour regular for a decade during which time he has won more than £1 million, Peter is not one of sports' most imposing physical presences. Indeed, a few years back he modestly proclaimed, 'If Greg Norman is the Great White Shark, I am the Little Fat Fish Finger.'

Senior shares a pawnbroking company back home in Brisbane with his brother, and there is no chance of Sam Torrance redeeming the broom-handle putter he gave the little Aussie three years ago. Peter readily admits that Sam's generosity and the putter saved his career. He had moved into contention with rounds of 66, 69 and 70. That 70 included brushing in a 30-foot eagle putt on the 530-yard seventh hole.

'I·now have a crack at it tomorrow,' said Senior. 'Three shots is nothing.'

It is now history that all were devoured by Norman's astonishing last-round 64, a round of golf praised to the heavens by Langer.

The 122nd Open at Royal St George's was a vintage championship. Yet how often since has Faldo gone to bed pondering the last time an Open champion shared the lead going into the final round, shot 67 and still lost by two. Langer also shot 67, including a 7 at the 14th, where he abandoned his rigid tactical plan, reached for his driver and drove out of bounds. Another last-day 67 shooter was Senior. All in vain. And Pavin's closing par 70 was a meritorious performance.

Any sub-70 round from a player in contention on the last day of a major championship is a considerable and highly praiseworthy achievement. Yet it happened that in 1993 a 67 was not good enough, not even for the world's No. 1 golfer and defending champion. Funny old game.

Greg Norman set the record with a 267 aggregate. He equalled records for the best first and final rounds by a champion.

NORMAN REGAINS THE PINNACLE

BY ROBERT SOMMERS

If it is true that the quality of any golf course is measured best by the quality of the players who rise to the top in the serious competitions staged over its grounds, then Royal St George's must stand very high in the rankings. With only a few exceptions, the group that led the 122nd Open Championship into the fourth round comprised the best players in the game.

As the day began under lowering skies and the threat of still more rain, 11 men stood within five strokes of one another. Nick Faldo and Corey Pavin shared first place, followed by Greg Norman and Bernhard Langer, then Nick Price, Peter Senior, Wayne Grady, Ernie Els, Fred Couples, John Daly and Fuzzy Zoeller.

It was an Aussie day.

Drawn from golfers from throughout the world, these included the top five on the Sony Ranking list and eight members of this extraordinary group represented winners of 14 of the game's four principle competitions — four Opens, one US Open, six US Masters and three USPGA Championships.

With three Opens and two US Masters, Faldo had won more than any of the others. Langer had won two US Masters, Couples one, and Zoeller a US Open and a US Masters. Grady, Daly and Price had won the USPGA, and Norman had won the 1986 Open. Of the leading 11, only Pavin, Senior and Els hadn't won on the big occasion.

No one could recall seeing such a stunning leaderboard. With so many clustered so closely together, a tight, spirited battle seemed inevitable.

Those predictions were realized, for we were about to embark on a day like few in this old championship's memory, a wild and wonderful day of exquis-

ite shotmaking, incredible scoring and a triumphal march down the broad, grandstand-lined avenue of the final hole by Norman, who once again climbed to the peak of the game after toppling during the previous few years.

It was a day that saw the young South African Els become the first man in the Open's history to score four rounds in the 60s and yet place no higher than a tie for sixth place; a day in which 27 men broke par for a record total of 116 for the championship; a day that saw Iain Pyman, the Amateur champion, shoot 281, the lowest score ever by an amateur in the Open; and a day when Paul Lawrie, a young newcomer to the European Tour, drew lusty cheers from the throng lining the 17th by holing a full-blooded three iron for an eagle 2 on his way to a round of 65 that lifted him into a tie for sixth place.

It was a day that began with Payne Stewart, far out of the race at first, ripping around Royal St George's in 63 strokes, equalling the record low Open score that had been matched earlier in the week by Faldo, and that ended with Norman shooting 64, and with 267 breaking Tom Watson's inviolable record of 268, then, when it was done, stating flatly, 'I am in awe of myself.'

No one could remember a day quite like it with so many of the game's great names playing their absolute best, turning the championship into a test of nerve as well as astounding golf. Langer demonstrated once again his fighting qualities, struggling back from another double bogey — this at the 14th where he drove out of bounds — and battling back into contention by birdieing the next two holes.

Paul Lawrie's 65 was 'the biggest day of my career.'

Payne Stewart's 63 equalled the 18-hole record.

A final 66 lifted Scott Simpson to joint ninth.

Peter Senior was joint fourth with three late birdies.

Corey Pavin never caught up after bogeys on the first and fourth holes. He was joint fourth.

Then there was Faldo trying for a consecutive Open, the fourth of his career, beginning the round a stroke ahead of Norman, shooting a superb 67 under enormous tension, and yet losing by two strokes.

The whole day left those who played such extraordinary golf, as well as those who only watched it, emotionally limp and yet exhilarated. We must wait to see if its memory will live as long as recollections of that wonderful year of 1977 at Turnberry when Watson and Jack Nicklaus matched stroke for stroke through the final 36 holes, Watson winning with 65-65 against Nicklaus's 65-66, or perhaps the last wrenching round at Royal Lytham and St Annes in 1988, when Seve Ballesteros and Price played one glorious shot after another until Ballesteros finally won on the home green. The afternoon at Sandwich certainly is a candidate.

The round had hardly begun when Stewart started working his miracles. The 1991 US Open champion and a winner of the USPGA Championship before then, Stewart had often played well in the Open, placing second to Sandy Lyle at Sandwich in 1985, and to Faldo at St Andrews in 1990. Runner-up to Lee Janzen in the US Open a month earlier, Stewart had shot what appeared to be reasonable scores of 71, 72 and 70 at Sandwich, but with 213 for 54 holes, he had been left far behind, 11 strokes behind Faldo and Pavin, the co-leaders.

Playing superb approaches and putting like a man possessed, Stewart birdied four holes on the first nine, dropping a 50-foot putt on the fifth, and raced to the turn in 31.

Coming back he holed from 20 feet on the 13th and from six feet on the 14th. Six under par now, he pulled his putt and missed from 15 feet once again at the 15th, but on that difficult and demanding 17th, Stewart played a wonderful six iron within 10 feet and holed the putt for his seventh birdie of the round.

One more birdie would break the Open's 18-hole record. Stewart drilled a long drive and followed with a four iron to 25 feet. For a heart-stopping moment his putt looked as if it might fall for the 62, but it veered away and Stewart shot 63. He had finished with 276, four under par, but only a miracle could make it mean something.

Rain had fallen heavily since Stewart had reached the 15th, and a chilly wind blustered in from the Channel. Soon, though, by the time the leaders stepped on to the first tee, the rainclouds had drifted off and patches of sky showed through the overcast. The drama was about to begin.

Everyone knew that whoever was to win this Open would have to beat Faldo, for no one in the game is more dangerous or more intimidating with an important championship at stake, especially when he holds or shares the lead. The result would depend on

Ernie Els (left) and Nick Price (right) both broke par, but were joint sixth.

how his challengers would hold up under the unrelenting pressure he was sure to apply.

Norman was paired with Langer in the next-to-last group, followed by Faldo and Pavin. Many of those who remembered the Saturday round at St Andrews three years earlier felt Norman had the most to prove, for Faldo had embarrassed him that afternoon. Greg had played two superb rounds of 66 while Faldo had shot 67 and 65; but on that mild and pleasant day, Faldo had shot another 67, and in the face of that superb round, Norman had struggled to 76. Greg had not been the same since. This, then, was his time for reprisal.

Greg wasted no time sparring; he attacked from the first stroke, nailing a driver into centre fairway, lofting a nine iron within nine feet, and holing the putt. At the same time, Langer rolled in a 20-footer for a birdie of his own. Both men slipped to eight under par, tied with Faldo and Pavin. Moments later Pavin played a terrible approach, missing the first green by miles, bogeyed, and fell one stroke behind.

Not playing up to the standards he had set earlier in the week, he would never catch up, although he bounced back right away by birdieing the second. A second bogey at the fourth cost him another stroke, and although he hung around the fringes, he never again played a significant part.

Faldo, meantime, played a gorgeous pitch to the second that almost fell into the hole. His birdie dropped him to nine under par just after Norman drilled a four iron dead at the flagstick on the third and holed from 25 feet. Both men stood at nine under par now.

Faldo fell behind on the fourth by missing the type of putt he never misses when it matters. His approach ran over the back and his chip hit the hole and lipped out, spinning about five feet away. His putt for the par hit the hole again and once more spun out again. A bogey 5 and back to eight under. Stunned, his gallery groaned.

Faldo fought back, playing a nice six iron on the sixth and birdieing, but Norman had already made

Bernhard Langer putted for seven birdies.

Greg Norman holed from 25 feet at the third.

his own birdie there, dropping to 10 under par, still a stroke ahead.

Three under for the round now, Norman missed a great chance to birdie, or perhaps eagle, the seventh. His four-iron second ran on to the green, but the radical contours turned the ball away, off the side and down a gentle slope.

Taking his putter, Norman rapped his ball a touch too gently; it climbed the slope but lost momentum near the crest, hung for an instant, then rolled back down again. A stroke wasted. Once again Greg rapped the ball with his putter, this time hard enough to roll on to the green a few feet from the cup. He holed the putt, saving a par 5, but this was a hole he should have birdied.

While he had given away one stroke to the field, it didn't matter to the outcome of the championship, for moments later Faldo parred the seventh as well, driving into a fairway bunker, hitting the top of the bunker face with his recovery, and leaving it in the rough no more than 30 yards farther on. A pitch and

two putts and Nick too had his 5.

Langer, meantime, birdied, picking up a stroke on both men.

Now Norman led at 10 under par, with Faldo and Langer one stroke behind at nine under, and Pavin two strokes further back at seven under, along with Price, who had gone out in 33. Five men stood within three strokes of one another with 10 holes to play.

Quickly, though, Norman pulled further ahead. After a struggling par on the eighth, he lofted a 135-yard nine iron to six feet on the ninth for his fourth birdie of the day. Out in 31, he had fallen to 11 under par and opened a lead of two strokes over both Faldo and Langer.

Only Norman, Faldo and Langer mattered now. Price had stumbled, bogeying the 10th, 11th and 12th; Pavin could make no headway at all, and Senior had waited too long to make his move.

The wind had picked up strength, scattering the clouds, and the sun broke through the overcast, tak-

Nick Faldo saved par at the 13th after driving into a bunker.

ing much of the chill from the air. The great gallery had broken into two groups, one moving with Norman and Langer, the other lagging behind, cheering on Faldo, urging him on in his pursuit of that fourth Open Championship. With each succeeding hole, though, Nick's hope grew dimmer. Playing flawless golf, Norman was giving him no opening. Nick would have to make birdies.

When Faldo did birdie, he did it with flair. His tee shot to the 11th, a strong 216-yard par 3 playing toward the glittering waters of Pegwell Bay, rose in the sunlit sky, dropped dead on line to the hole, and hit the flagstick. With better luck he could have holed in one, but his ball ran a few feet past the hole, and the putt fell.

Ten under par after the birdie fell, Faldo had picked up no ground, for Norman played a marvellous sand wedge to four feet on the 12th, and the ball could do nothing but fall. Twelve under now, five under for the round, and still two strokes ahead of both Faldo and Langer, who suddenly began making birdies.

After bogeying the 11th and dropping three strokes behind, Langer had played an even better pitch to the 12th, a foot inside Norman's, and matched Greg's birdie. Not through yet, he added another at the 13th, playing a 443-yard hole with a driver and

pitching wedge to eight feet. Now Langer stood 10 under par, two strokes behind, with the 14th, a certified birdie hole, coming up.

Here he made another major mistake, like his double bogey from the hawthorn bush the previous day.

The 14th runs alongside Prince's, the neighbouring course where Gene Sarazen had won the Open 61 years earlier. Prince's is out of bounds. Langer made a bad swing and pushed his ball beyond the white stakes marking the boundary. Langer was shaken, of course, and the gallery wondered how his bad drive might affect Norman. Watching Langer play such a bad shot might cause him to play a cautious shot. But Greg had been playing better than he had ever played, hadn't mis-hit a shot all day, and had missed only one fairway in two rounds.

Trusting his swing, Greg ripped his drive far and true down the fairway. A three wood into the light rough lining the right of the fairway, and then a precise pitch nearly fell into the cup. It rolled only inches away, Norman tapped it in, and he had his sixth birdie of the round.

Langer finished the hole in 7, another double bogey, and dropped five strokes behind, back to eight under par. Norman stood 13 under par now, three strokes ahead of Faldo. Only his own collapse could change the result.

Still Faldo fought on; he wouldn't give up until the holes had run out. While Norman strode down the 15th fairway, Nick birdied the 14th. Eleven under par now, still two strokes behind, he had to have Norman's help to catch up.

He nearly had it at the 15th. After another long and straight drive, Greg's six iron slipped off the edge of the green and rolled down a steep slope. Since the ball lay in fairway-height grass, Norman putted up the slope toward the hole. Suddenly the ball swerved off line, curled away from the hole, and rolled 10 feet away.

This would be no easy putt; it could mean a lost stroke and the opening Faldo needed. Still confident,

Faldo maintained the pressure with four birdies.

After this putt at the 15th, Norman made a 10-footer.

Norman added a four-foot birdie at the 16th.

Norman rolled his ball into the cup. Moments later he struck a magnificent five iron to the heart of the 16th green, within four feet of the hole, and added another birdie. Greg had gone 14 under par for 70 holes, and seven under par for the round. Two more pars and he would shoot 63.

Now Norman had put the championship out of Faldo's reach, but we still had a struggle for second place, and Langer was striking back. After his 7 on the 14th, he played a wonderful four iron to 10 feet on the 15th and a five iron to 20 feet on the 16th. He holed both putts and moved back to 10 under par, challenging Faldo for second place. If Nick should slip, Bernhard might catch him.

Perhaps overconfident by then, Norman made a mistake on the 17th. Reaching the back of the green with his approach, he putted within a foot and a half, but then, perhaps carelessly, he lipped out, losing one stroke of his lead. He said later he couldn't remember ever missing so short a putt.

It didn't really matter, though. His long blond hair ruffling in the wind, Norman drilled a perfect drive down the 18th and struck a perfectly played four iron to 18 feet. He had won the championship.

Langer appreciated what he had just seen even more than the gallery. As he and Norman strode through the wildly cheering crowd, he moved to Greg's side and told him, 'That was the greatest golf I've ever seen in my life. You deserve to win.'

Norman had hit every shot squarely on the face of

This may have been a championship won with his driver, and Norman drilled a perfect shot on the 72nd hole.

Langer joined the applause for Norman, as they approached the 18th green with Norman holding a two-stroke lead.

the club, hit every fairway, and the four greens he missed cost him nothing, except for a possible birdie on the seventh. He shot 64 for the round, which, combined with his earlier rounds of 66, 68 and 69, added up to a 72-hole score of 267. He had played every round in the 60s, becoming the first Open champion ever to do so, and had beaten Faldo by two strokes and Langer by three.

Fighting to the end, Nick had played the 15th through the 17th flawlessly and even at the end, with the championship out of reach, he refused to yield. He pulled his drive on the 18th close to the metal fence holding back the gallery, chopped his ball from the wild rough well short of the green, and pitched perhaps 15 feet from the cup.

There would be no Open Championship now, but he needed this putt to secure second place. It never occurred to him to do anything but try his best to hole the putt. He studied the line, took his time, and in a demonstration of championship style, he willed the ball into the hole, ending a day that must rank among the greatest the old game has ever known.

Norman was off in a red Rolls with the trophy.

Before the massive crowd at the final green, Norman studied the 18 feet between him and a second Open victory.

FOURTH ROUND RESULTS

HOLE	1	2	3	4	5	6	7	8	9	10	11	12	13	14	15	16	17	18	
PAR	4	4	3	4	4	3	5	4	4	4	3	4	4	5	4	3	4	4	TOTAL
Greg Norman	3	4	2	4	4	2	5	4	3	4	3	3	4	4	4	2	5	4	64-267
Nick Faldo	4	3	3	5	4	2	5	4	4	4	2	4	4	4	4	3	4	4	67-269
Bernhard Langer	3	4	3	5	3	3	4	4	4	4	4	3	3	7	3	2	4	4	67-270
Peter Senior	5	4	3	4	4	3	4	4	4	3	3	4	4	4	3	2	4	5	67-272
Corey Pavin	5	3	3	5	4	4	4	4	4	4	4	3	4	4	3	3	5	4	70-272
Paul Lawrie	4	3	3	4	4	3	5	4	3	4	2	4	4	4	4	3	2	5	65-274
Ernie Els	3	5	3	4	4	3	4	4	4	3	4	3	4	4	4	3	4	5	68-274
Nick Price	4	3	3	4	3	3	5	5	3	5	4	5	4	4	4	3	3	4	69-274
Scott Simpson	3	4	3	5	4	2	4	4	4	4	3	3	4	5	4	2	4	4	66-275
Fred Couples	4	4	3	4	4	2	5	4	4	4	3	3	4	4	4	3	5	5	69-275
Wayne Grady	4	4	3	5	5	3	3	5	4	4	3	4	3	5	4	2	4	4	69-275
Payne Stewart	4	3	3	4	3	3	4	4	3	4	3	4	3	4	4	3	3	4	63-276

HOLE SUMMARY

HOLE	PAR	EAGLES	BIRDIES	PARS	BOGEYS	HIGHER	RANK	AVERAGE
1	4	0	15	51	12	0	11	3.96
2	4	0	16	52	7	3	11	3.96
3	3	0	12	49	15	2	7	3.09
4	4	0	2	40	31	5	1	4.50
5	4	0	12	51	13	2	9	4.06
6	3	0	22	49	7	0	17	2.81
7	5	2	47	28	1	0	18	4.36
8	4	0	4	51	21	2	4	4.27
9	4	0	15	53	9	1	13	3.95
OUT	35	2	145	424	116	15		34.96
10	4	0	10	48	16	4	5	4.18
11	3	0	11	49	18	0	7	3.09
12	4	0	28	40	9	1	16	3.78
13	4	0	11	55	12	0	10	4.01
14	5	0	28	36	8	6	14	4.92
15	4	0	6	50	17	5	3	4.28
16	3	0	17	55	6	0	15	2.86
17	4	1	6	55	14	2	6	4.13
18	4	0	4	48	22	4	2	4.33
IN	35	1	121	436	122	22		35.58
TOTAL	70	3	266	860	238	37		70.54

Players Below Par	27
Players At Par	14
Players Above Par	37

LOW SCORES

Low First Nine	Paul Broadhurst	31
	John Huston	31
	Greg Norman	31
	Mark Roe	31
	Payne Stewart	31
Low Second Nine	Tom Kite	32
	Paul Lawrie	32
	Jesper Parnevik	32
	Peter Senior	32
	Payne Stewart	32
Low Round	Payne Stewart	63

CHAMPIONSHIP HOLE SUMMARY

HOLE	PAR	EAGLES	BIRDIES	PARS	BOGEYS	HIGHER	RANK	AVERAGE
1	4	0	66	316	81	5	12	4.05
2	4	0	89	337	34	8	17	3.92
3	3	0	39	298	121	10	3	3.22
4	4	0	17	255	165	31	1	4.46
5	4	0	46	343	73	6	10	4.08
6	3	0	84	311	69	4	13	2.99
7	5	25	266	163	14	0	18	4.35
8	4	0	38	285	134	11	4	4.25
9	4	0	60	317	81	10	9	4.09
OUT	35	25	705	2625	772	85		35.41
10	4	0	51	301	100	16	8	4.18
11	3	0	38	315	110	5	6	3.18
12	4	0	83	317	64	4	14	3.98
13	4	1	71	303	86	7	11	4.06
14	5	0	122	275	49	22	15	4.95
15	4	0	41	309	103	15	7	4.20
16	3	0	80	326	60	2	15	2.97
17	4	1	32	296	126	13	4	4.25
18	4	0	20	271	156	21	2	4.38
IN	35	2	538	2713	854	105		36.15
TOTAL	70	27	1243	5338	1626	190		71.56

	FIRST ROUND	SECOND ROUND	THIRD ROUND	FOURTH ROUND	TOTAL
Players Below Par	47	26	16	27	116
Players At Par	22	16	13	14	65
Players Above Par	87	114	49	37	287

ATTENDANCE

PRACTICE ROUNDS	22,000
FIRST ROUND	25,000
SECOND ROUND	34,000
THIRD ROUND	31,000
FOURTH ROUND	29,000
TOTAL	141,000

Greg Norman wrestled Royal St George's into submission with an awe-inspiring display of golf.

WELL WORTH THE WAIT

BY JOHN HOPKINS

We categorize our heroes and heroines on the basis on one incident, one anecdote. The single moment that defines them in our mind's eye may be unfair or inaccurate but it remains just that, the moment on which we base our feelings for that person. Thus, Tom Kite is the man who left an uphill putt short on the 68th hole of a US Masters when to have holed it would have given him the lead. Thus, Seve Ballesteros is the man who hits his tee shots into car parks. And thus, for me, Greg Norman is the game's most gracious loser. Or was until Sunday, 18th July 1993.

It was at the Johnnie Walker World Championship in Jamaica in 1992 that the moment occurred. Norman had just missed a three-foot putt and lost a play-off to Nick Faldo. All the old ghosts were hovering: the spectres of 1986 when he had led after 54 holes of all four major championships and won only one; of his driving into a bunker in the play-off for the 1989 Open; of all the other occasions when Norman had been about to win, only to lose. Almost any golfer in the world would have wanted time to compose himself after having Faldo snatch the championship from him. No more than one minute after signing his card and shaking Faldo's hand, Norman had agreed to be interviewed by television and radio. What stoicism, I thought, at the same time as I was wondering for the umpteenth time whether such gentlemanliness in defeat was diminishing his chances of victory?

A red, raw streak of nerve was exposed briefly when Norman said to the interviewer, 'I'll talk but don't cut me, understand,' meaning he didn't want any more 'There you go again, Greg, snatching defeat from the jaws of victory' type of questions. But

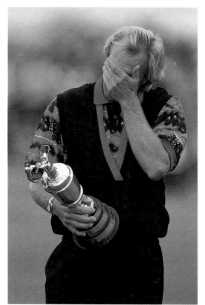
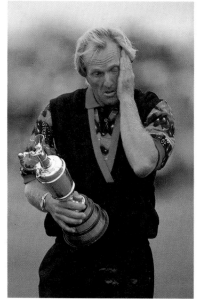

Norman was briefly overcome by emotion when he accepted the prized claret jug.

It was 'Well Done Greg' — and in 1994 Norman will return to the venue of his 1986 victory.

that was all. He had lost. It was time to face the next challenge, to hold his head up high, to find merit even in defeat.

Is this the incident by which I remember Norman? Partly, but not entirely. A few years ago I was anxious to talk to him after his wonderful round at Doral, 62 I think, on the famed and feared Blue Monster course. I tracked him down to the Far East but kept missing him as he made his way home again. Messages were left in hotels across Asia but the return calls never came. Then one morning the telephone rang, and after I had answered it, a familiar voice said: 'This is Greg Norman. I tried you a couples of times but there was no reply.' We talked for 15 minutes about his round, his thoughts about the upcoming US Masters, about himself. He could not have been more helpful. If, as was later suggested, he was talking to me on his car telephone while driving near his home in Florida, then that increased the level of my gratitude.

The telephone incident with Norman was brought into focus a couple of years later. The then-current US Open champion was at home when my request to interview him prior to the Open was relayed to him by his management company. 'Give me your telephone number,' his manager had said. 'He is quite good about calling back. If he has time I'm sure he'll do so.' Nothing happened for three days and then around 11.30 one morning the telephone rang. When I answered it the operator asked if mine was the number he had dialled. I said it was. 'Will you accept a reverse charge call from America?' he asked. I suppose I shouldn't have been surprised. A fellow journalist once received a reverse charge call from a player 15 miles away.

All this came to mind on this Sunday in July as Norman played the round of golf he has shown himself to be capable of playing many times but never to win a major championship. Was this to be Norman's Open? It was. This time Norman proved that nice guys can be winners and that he can win by beating the best players in the world. He played 63 near-perfect strokes on this day, one missed 14-inch putt being his only blemish. No one backed off to give him the 122nd Open. No one folded. He went out and, as he has threatened to do so many times around the world, he wrestled this course into submission with an awe-inspiring display of golf.

Bernhard Langer said as much, not me. As he and Norman walked up the 18th, their 72nd hole, as Norman was leading by two strokes, Langer said: 'That was the greatest golf I have ever seen in my life. You deserve to win.'

His most challenging moment might have been on the 14th tee when he watched Langer, his playing partner, drive over a fence separating Royal St George's from Prince's. A man waving a red flag indicated it was out of bounds. In the past Norman has had a tendency to block shots out to the right when under pressure. If ever he was under pressure it was now, with the world's two best players breathing down his neck. He could have been excused if he had taken a one iron for safety from the tee and smashed his ball an enormous distance down the fairway into the prime position from which to attack the green.

By doubling the total of his major championships, Norman saved his career, indeed perhaps jump-started the second phase of it. Three years earlier, after Robert Gamez had holed a full seven iron from the 72nd fairway of Bay Hill and David Frost had holed from a bunker on the 72nd hole at New Orleans, both to snatch victory from under Norman's beaky nose, Norman had explained what his philosophy was. 'I've developed the ability to blot crappy

Norman watched his approach shot to the 72nd hole.

things out of my mind,' he said. 'It doesn't matter whether it's on or off the course. There is no point in stewing over them. If I hit a bad shot five minutes ago, I say, "Hey, that never happened." I've taught myself that over the years. I have always been a believer in being positive. Never have anything that is negative. That's true of life and also on the golf course. If I screw up myself I can get mad at myself. When somebody does it to you, forget about it.'

He went on to say why he was looking at the new decade with such enthusiasm. 'I look at the 1980s as a complete learning experience. I feel like I've just turned the front nine and shot about 33. I'm looking to shoot 31 or 30 on the back nine.' For a while, though, he looked as though he would struggle to break 40. No matter that his attitude was magnificently optimistic; in private he was depressed. He was making a huge amount of money off the course

Norman's gallery included (from left) wife Laura, friend Frank Williams and coach Butch Harmon.

but not fulfilling his enormous potential on it. 'I was thinking of concentrating on designing golf courses,' he said. 'I was as low as can be. I was ready to quit.'

Whoever said it was darkest before dawn was right. Cliches often are. That's why they become cliches. One day in 1992 Norman examined himself in the mirror. 'What do you want to do?' he asked the face that stared out at him. 'Give up the game or fight back and be the best you can be?' The answer was he wanted to regain the form he had shown in the late 80s. There and then he decided to re-dedicate himself to golf. 'I love to play golf,' he said once. 'The question of winning will be decided by my own level of commitment.'

Just as Faldo had gone to David Leadbetter in the mid-80s to help him build a swing that would withstand the unyielding pressure of the closing holes of a major championship, so Norman went to Butch Harmon to have his swing overhauled. Harmon did not just give Norman a lick of paint. 'He changed everything,' Norman said. 'My swing, my putting, everything. A key swing change has tightened up my swing. I had been loose before, with my body not in sync with my swing. I tightened up my body rotation with Butch. That is why I have great control of distance and flight. All the things that should work together are now working together. I've worked harder than I did when I was 21 or 22.'

Norman himself noticed the change in the Open at Muirfield in 1992, when he started to receive positive feedback. That encouraged him to work still

A happy Greg and Laura Norman with the trophy.

harder. His results prior to this year's Open were nothing to write home about. They were patchy: a missed cut in the US Open and 33rd place in the US Masters to be set against a victory at Doral and second place in the Western Open, two weeks prior to Sandwich. Then he started the Open with a double-bogey 6. It was another occasion to be positive. Norman hitched up his trousers and got to work.

'I see myself as coming to my second decade,' he said. 'I've blown some winning positions and no doubt will do so again, but not so often. I am ready to attack the 90s. I am prepared for all the toil that will be necessary to meet the goals I've set myself for major championships. I will go through it all because I love to play golf and that's my work. Scuba diving is my pleasure. I am recovering my old aggression on the course. I know the rules. I live by the sword, so I must be prepared to die by the sword. But the time to judge me is not yet. I will be 46 at the end of this decade. Judgement day for Greg Norman the golfer will come in the year 2000.'

Between now and then will Norman win a third, fourth and fifth major title? I'll hedge my bets. I will only put my wife, my car, my house and my overdraft on his doing so. The game is not so strong it can do without the most exciting golfer since Ballesteros was in his prime; the longest, straightest driver since Jack Nicklaus; the greatest money earner in golf since Arnold Palmer. Golf needs the aura that is Greg Norman as much as Norman needs the opium that is golf. Well done, Greg. Good on yer, mate. It was a long time coming, but it was worth the wait.

Norman acknowledged the applause as he completed his final-round 64.

Sandy Lyle (1985) and Tony Jacklin (1969).

RECORDS OF THE OPEN CHAMPIONSHIP

MOST VICTORIES
6, Harry Vardon, 1896-98-99-1903-11-14
5, James Braid, 1901-05-06-08-10; J.H. Taylor, 1894-95-1900-09-13; Peter Thomson, 1954-55-56-58-65; Tom Watson, 1975-77-80-82-83

MOST TIMES RUNNER-UP OR JOINT RUNNER-UP
7, Jack Nicklaus, 1964-67-68-72-76-77-79
6, J.H. Taylor, 1896-1904-05-06-07-14

OLDEST WINNER
Old Tom Morris, 46 years 99 days, 1867
Roberto de Vicenzo, 44 years 93 days, 1967

YOUNGEST WINNER
Young Tom Morris, 17 years 5 months 8 days, 1868
Willie Auchterlonie, 21 years 24 days, 1893
Severiano Ballesteros, 22 years 3 months 12 days, 1979

YOUNGEST AND OLDEST COMPETITOR
John Ball, 14 years, 1878
Gene Sarazen, 71 years 4 months 13 days, 1973

BIGGEST MARGIN OF VICTORY
13 strokes, Old Tom Morris, 1862
12 strokes, Young Tom Morris, 1870
8 strokes, J.H. Taylor, 1900 and 1913; James Braid, 1908
6 strokes, Bobby Jones, 1927; Walter Hagen, 1929; Arnold Palmer, 1962; Johnny Miller, 1976

LOWEST WINNING AGGREGATES
267 (66, 68, 69, 64), Greg Norman, Royal St George's, 1993
268 (68, 70, 65, 65), Tom Watson, Turnberry, 1977
270 (67, 65, 67, 71), Nick Faldo, St Andrews, 1990
271 (68, 70, 64, 69), Tom Watson, Muirfield, 1980
272 (71, 71, 64, 66), Ian Baker-Finch, Royal Birkdale, 1991; (66, 64, 69, 73), Nick Faldo, Muirfield, 1992

LOWEST AGGREGATES BY RUNNER-UP
269 (68, 70, 65, 66), Jack Nicklaus, Turnberry, 1977; (69, 63, 70, 67), Nick Faldo, Royal St George's, 1993
273 (66, 67, 70, 70), John Cook, Muirfield, 1992
274 (68, 70, 69, 67), Mike Harwood, Royal Birkdale, 1991

LOWEST AGGREGATE BY AN AMATEUR
281 (68, 72, 70, 71), Iain Pyman, Royal St George's, 1993

LOWEST INDIVIDUAL ROUND
63, Mark Hayes, second round, Turnberry, 1977; Isao Aoki, third round, Muirfield, 1980; Greg Norman, second round, Turnberry, 1986; Paul Broadhurst, third round, St Andrews, 1990; Jodie Mudd, fourth round, Royal Birkdale, 1991; Nick Faldo, second round, and Payne Stewart, fourth round, Royal St George's, 1993

LOWEST INDIVIDUAL ROUND BY AN AMATEUR
66, Frank Stranahan, fourth round, Troon, 1950

LOWEST FIRST ROUND
64, Craig Stadler, Royal Birkdale, 1983; Christy O'Connor Jr., Royal St George's, 1985; Rodger Davis, Muirfield, 1987; Raymond Floyd and Steve Pate, Muirfield, 1992

LOWEST SECOND ROUND
63, Mark Hayes, Turnberry, 1977; Greg Norman, Turnberry, 1986; Nick Faldo, Royal St George's, 1993

LOWEST THIRD ROUND
63, Isao Aoki, Muirfield, 1980; Paul Broadhurst, St Andrews, 1990

LOWEST FOURTH ROUND
63, Jodie Mudd, Royal Birkdale, 1991; Payne Stewart, Royal St George's, 1993

LOWEST FIRST 36 HOLES
130 (66, 64), Nick Faldo, Muirfield, 1992
132 (67, 65), Henry Cotton, Sandwich, 1934; (66, 66), Greg Norman and (67, 65), Nick Faldo, St Andrews, 1990; (69, 63), Nick Faldo, Royal St George's, 1993

LOWEST SECOND 36 HOLES
130 (65, 65), Tom Watson, Turnberry, 1977; (64, 66), Ian Baker-Finch, Royal Birkdale, 1991

LOWEST FIRST 54 HOLES
199 (67, 65, 67), Nick Faldo, St Andrews, 1990; (66, 64, 69), Nick Faldo, Muirfield, 1992

LOWEST FINAL 54 HOLES
200 (70, 65, 65), Tom Watson, Turnberry, 1977; (63, 70, 67), Nick Faldo, Royal St George's, 1993
201 (71, 64, 66), Ian Baker-Finch, Royal Birkdale, 1991; (68, 69, 64), Greg Norman and (68, 64, 69), Wayne Grady, Royal St George's, 1993

LOWEST 9 HOLES
28, Denis Durnian, first 9, Royal Birkdale, 1983
29, Peter Thomson and Tom Haliburton, first 9, Royal Lytham, 1958; Tony Jacklin, first 9, St Andrews, 1970; Bill Longmuir, first 9, Royal Lytham, 1979; David J. Russell, first 9, Royal Lytham, 1988; Ian Baker-Finch and Paul Broadhurst, first 9, St Andrews, 1990; Ian Baker-Finch, first 9, Royal Birkdale, 1991

CHAMPIONS IN THREE DECADES
Harry Vardon, 1896, 1903, 1911
J.H. Taylor, 1894, 1900, 1913
Gary Player, 1959, 1968, 1974

BIGGEST SPAN BETWEEN FIRST AND LAST VICTORIES
19 years, J.H. Taylor, 1894-1913
18 years, Harry Vardon, 1896-1914
15 years, Gary Player, 1959-74
14 years, Henry Cotton, 1934-48

SUCCESSIVE VICTORIES
4, Young Tom Morris, 1868-72. No championship in 1871
3, Jamie Anderson, 1877-79; Bob Ferguson, 1880-82, Peter Thomson, 1954-56
2, Old Tom Morris, 1861-62; J.H. Taylor, 1894-95; Harry Vardon, 1898-99; James Braid, 1905-06; Bobby Jones, 1926-27; Walter Hagen, 1928-29; Bobby Locke, 1949-50; Arnold Palmer, 1961-62; Lee Trevino, 1971-72; Tom Watson, 1982-83

VICTORIES BY AMATEURS
3, Bobby Jones, 1926-27-30
2, Harold Hilton, 1892-97
1, John Ball, 1890
Roger Wethered lost a play-off in 1921

HIGHEST NUMBER OF TOP FIVE FINISHES
16, J.H. Taylor, Jack Nicklaus
15, Harry Vardon, James Braid

HIGHEST NUMBER OF ROUNDS UNDER 70
31, Jack Nicklaus
27, Nick Faldo
23, Tom Watson
21, Lee Trevino
18, Severiano Ballesteros
17, Greg Norman
16, Bernhard Langer
15, Peter Thomson
14, Gary Player
13, Ben Crenshaw
12, Bobby Locke, Arnold Palmer, Payne Stewart

OUTRIGHT LEADER AFTER EVERY ROUND
Willie Auchterlonie, 1893; J.H. Taylor, 1894 and 1900; James Braid, 1908; Ted Ray, 1912; Bobby Jones, 1927; Gene Sarazen, 1932; Henry Cotton, 1934; Tom Weiskopf, 1973

RECORD LEADS (SINCE 1892)
After 18 holes:
4 strokes, James Braid, 1908; Bobby Jones, 1927; Henry Cotton, 1934; Christy O'Connor Jr., 1985

After 36 holes:
9 strokes, Henry Cotton, 1934
After 54 holes:
10 strokes, Henry Cotton, 1934
7 strokes, Tony Lema, 1964
6 strokes, James Braid, 1908
5 strokes, Arnold Palmer, 1962; Bill Rogers, 1981; Nick Faldo, 1990

CHAMPIONS WITH EACH ROUND LOWER THAN PREVIOUS ONE
Jack White, 1904, Sandwich, 80, 75, 72, 69
James Braid, 1906, Muirfield, 77, 76, 74, 73
Ben Hogan, 1953, Carnoustie, 73, 71, 70, 68
Gary Player, 1959, Muirfield, 75, 71, 70, 68

CHAMPION WITH FOUR ROUNDS THE SAME
Densmore Shute, 1933, St Andrews, 73, 73, 73, 73 (excluding the play-off)

BIGGEST VARIATION BETWEEN ROUNDS OF A CHAMPION
14 strokes, Henry Cotton, 1934, second round 65, fourth round 79
11 strokes, Jack White, 1904, first round 80, fourth round 69; Greg Norman, 1986, first round 74, second round 63, third round 74

BIGGEST VARIATION BETWEEN TWO ROUNDS
17 strokes, Jack Nicklaus, 1981, first round 83, second round 66; Ian Baker-Finch, 1986, first round 86, second round 69

BEST COMEBACK BY CHAMPIONS
After 18 holes:
Harry Vardon, 1896, 11 strokes behind the leader
After 36 holes:
George Duncan, 1920, 13 strokes behind the leader
After 54 holes:
Jim Barnes, 1925, 5 strokes behind the leader
Of non-champions, Greg Norman, 1989, 7 strokes behind the leader and lost in a play-off

CHAMPIONS WITH FOUR ROUNDS UNDER 70
Greg Norman, 1993, Royal St George's, 66, 68, 69, 64
Of non-champions:
Ernie Els, 1993, Royal St George's, 68, 69, 69, 68

BEST FINISHING ROUND BY A CHAMPION
64, Greg Norman, Royal St George's, 1993
65, Tom Watson, Turnberry, 1977; Severiano Ballesteros, Royal Lytham, 1988
66, Johnny Miller, Royal Birkdale, 1976; Ian Baker-Finch, Royal Birkdale, 1991

WORST FINISHING ROUND BY A CHAMPION SINCE 1920
79, Henry Cotton, Sandwich, 1934
78, Reg Whitcombe, Sandwich, 1938
77, Walter Hagen, Hoylake, 1924

WORST OPENING ROUND BY A CHAMPION SINCE 1919

80, George Duncan, Deal, 1920 (he also had a second round of 80)
77, Walter Hagen, Hoylake, 1924

BEST OPENING ROUND BY A CHAMPION

66, Peter Thomson, Royal Lytham, 1958; Nick Faldo, Muirfield, 1992; Greg Norman, Royal St George's, 1993
67, Henry Cotton, Sandwich, 1934; Tom Watson, Royal Birkdale, 1983; Severiano Ballesteros, Royal Lytham, 1988; Nick Faldo, St Andrews, 1990

BIGGEST RECOVERY IN 18 HOLES BY A CHAMPION

George Duncan, Deal, 1920, was 13 strokes behind the leader, Abe Mitchell, after 36 holes and level after 54

MOST APPEARANCES ON FINAL DAY (SINCE 1892)

30, J.H. Taylor
29, Jack Nicklaus
27, Harry Vardon, James Braid
26, Peter Thomson
25, Gary Player
23, Dai Rees
22, Henry Cotton

CHAMPIONSHIP WITH HIGHEST NUMBER OF ROUNDS UNDER 70

116, Royal St George's, 1993

CHAMPIONSHIP SINCE 1946 WITH THE FEWEST ROUNDS UNDER 70

St Andrews, 1946; Hoylake, 1947; Portrush, 1951; Hoylake, 1956; Carnoustie, 1968. All had only two rounds under 70

LONGEST COURSE

Carnoustie, 1968, 7252 yd (6631 m)

COURSES MOST OFTEN USED

St Andrews and Prestwick, 24; Muirfield, 14; Sandwich, 12; Hoylake, 10; Royal Lytham, 8; Royal Birkdale, 7; Musselburgh, and Royal Troon, 6; Carnoustie, 5; Deal and Turnberry, 2; Royal Portrush and Prince's, 1

PRIZE MONEY

Year	Total	First Prize
1860	nil	nil
1863	10	nil
1864	16	6
1876	20	20
1889	22	8
1891	28.50	10
1892	110	(Amateur winner)
1893	100	30
1910	125	50
1920	225	75
1927	275	100
1930	400	100
1931	500	100
1946	1,000	150
1949	1,700	300
1953	2,450	500
1954	3,500	750
1955	3,750	1,000
1958	4,850	1,000
1959	5,000	1,000
1960	7,000	1,250
1961	8,500	1,400
1963	8,500	1,500
1965	10,000	1,750
1966	15,000	2,100
1968	20,000	3,000
1969	30,000	4,250
1970	40,000	5,250
1971	45,000	5,500
1972	50,000	5,500
1975	75,000	7,500
1977	100,000	10,000
1978	125,000	12,500
1979	155,000	15,500
1980	200,000	25,000
1982	250,000	32,000
1983	300,000	40,000
1984	451,000	55,000
1985	530,000	65,000
1986	600,000	70,000
1987	650,000	75,000
1988	700,000	80,000
1989	750,000	80,000
1990	825,000	85,000
1991	900,000	90,000
1992	950,000	95,000
1993	1,000,000	100,000

ATTENDANCE

Year	Attendance
1962	37,098
1963	24,585
1964	35,954
1965	32,927
1966	40,182
1967	29,880
1968	51,819
1969	46,001
1970	81,593
1971	70,076
1972	84,746
1973	78,810
1974	92,796
1975	85,258
1976	92,021
1977	87,615
1978	125,271
1979	134,501
1980	131,610
1981	111,987
1982	133,299
1983	142,892
1984	193,126
1985	141,619
1986	134,261
1987	139,189
1988	191,334
1989	160,639
1990	208,680
1991	189,435
1992	146,427
1993	141,000

Seve Ballesteros (1979, 1984, 1988)

Gene Sarazen (1932) and Greg Norman (1986, 1993)   Tom Watson (1975, 1977, 1980, 1982, 1983)

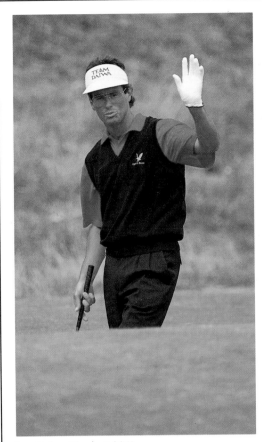

Ian Baker-Finch (1991)

Gary Player (1959, 1968, 1974)

Mark Calcavecchia (1989)

Jack Nicklaus (1966, 1970, 1978) and six times runner-up.

PAST RESULTS

* Denotes amateurs

1860 PRESTWICK

Willie Park, Musselburgh	55	59	60	174
Tom Morris Sr, Prestwick	58	59	59	176
Andrew Strath, St Andrews				180
Robert Andrew, Perth				191
George Brown, Blackheath				192

1861 PRESTWICK

Tom Morris Sr, Prestwick	54	56	53	163
Willie Park, Musselburgh	54	54	59	167
William Dow, Musselburgh	59	58	54	171
David Park, Musselburgh	58	57	57	172
Robert Andrew, Perth	58	61	56	175

1862 PRESTWICK

Tom Morris Sr, Prestwick	52	55	56	163
Willie Park, Musselburgh	59	59	58	176
Charles Hunter, Prestwick	60	60	58	178
William Dow, Musselburgh	60	58	63	181
* James Knight, Prestwick	62	61	63	186

1863 PRESTWICK

Willie Park, Musselburgh	56	54	58	168
Tom Morris Sr, Prestwick	56	58	56	170
David Park, Musselburgh	55	63	54	172
Andrew Strath, St Andrews	61	55	58	174
George Brown, St Andrews	58	61	57	176

1864 PRESTWICK

Tom Morris Sr, Prestwick	54	58	55	167
Andrew Strath, St Andrews	56	57	56	169
Robert Andrew, Perth	57	58	60	175
Willie Park, Musselburgh	55	67	55	177
William Dow, Musselburgh	56	58	67	181

1865 Prestwick

Andrew Strath, St Andrews	55	54	53	162
Willie Park, Musselburgh	56	52	56	164
William Dow, Musselburgh				171
Robert Kirk, St Andrews	64	54	55	173
Tom Morris Sr, St Andrews	57	61	56	174

1866 PRESTWICK

Willie Park, Musselburgh	54	56	59	169
David Park, Musselburgh	58	57	56	171
Robert Andrew, Perth	58	59	59	176
Tom Morris Sr, St Andrews	61	58	59	178
Robert Kirk, St Andrews	60	62	58	180

1867 PRESTWICK

Tom Morris Sr, St Andrews	58	54	58	170
Willie Park, Musselburgh	58	56	58	172
Andrew Strath, St Andrews	61	57	56	174
Tom Morris Jr, St Andrews	58	59	58	175
Robert Kirk, St Andrews	57	60	60	177

1868 PRESTWICK

Tom Morris Jr, St Andrews	50	55	52	157
Robert Andrew, Perth	53	54	52	159
Willie Park, Musselburgh	58	50	54	162
Robert Kirk, St Andrews	56	59	56	171
John Allen, Westward Ho!	54	52	63	172
Tom Morris Sr, St Andrews	56	62	58	176

1869 PRESTWICK

Tom Morris Jr, St Andrews	51	54	49	154
Tom Morris Sr, St Andrews	54	50	53	157
*S. Mure Fergusson, Royal and Ancient	57	54	54	165
Robert Kirk, St Andrews	53	58	57	168
David Strath, St Andrews	53	56	60	169
Jamie Anderson, St Andrews	60	56	57	173

1870 PRESTWICK

Tom Morris Jr, St Andrews	47	51	51	149
Bob Kirk, Royal Blackheath	52	52	57	161
David Strath, St Andrews	54	49	58	161
Tom Morris Sr, St Andrews	56	52	54	162
*William Doleman, Musselburgh	57	56	58	171
Willie Park, Musselburgh	60	55	58	173

1871 NO COMPETITION

1872 PRESTWICK

Tom Morris Jr, St Andrews	57	56	53	166
David Strath, St Andrews	56	52	61	169
*William Doleman, Musselburgh	63	60	54	177
Tom Morris Sr, St Andrews	62	60	57	179
David Park, Musselburgh	61	57	61	179

1873 ST ANDREWS

Tom Kidd, St Andrews	91	88	179
Jamie Anderson, St Andrews	91	89	180
Tom Morris Jr, St Andrews	94	89	183
Bob Kirk, Royal Blackheath	91	92	183
David Strath, St Andrews	97	90	187

1874 MUSSELBURGH

Mungo Park, Musselburgh	75	84	159
Tom Morris Jr, St Andrews	83	78	161
George Paxton, Musselburgh	80	82	162
Bob Martin, St Andrews	85	79	164
Jamie Anderson, St Andrews	82	83	165

1875 PRESTWICK

Willie Park, Musselburgh	56	59	51	166
Bob Martin, St Andrews	56	58	54	168
Mungo Park, Musselburgh	59	57	55	171
Robert Ferguson, Musselburgh	58	56	58	172
James Rennie, St Andrews	61	59	57	177

1876 ST ANDREWS

Bob Martin, St Andrews		86 90	176
David Strath, North Berwick		86 90	176
(Martin was awarded the title when Strath refused to play-off)			
Willie Park, Musselburgh		94 89	183
Tom Morris Sr, St Andrews		90 95	185
W. Thomson, Elie		90 95	185
Mungo Park, Musselburgh		95 90	185

1877 MUSSELBURGH

Jamie Anderson, St Andrews	40	42	37	41	160
Bob Pringle, Musselburgh	44	38	40	40	162
Bob Ferguson, Musselburgh	40	40	40	44	164
William Cosgrove, Musselburgh	41	39	44	40	164
David Strath, North Berwick	45	40	38	43	166
William Brown, Musselburgh	39	41	45	41	166

1878 PRESTWICK

Jamie Anderson, St Andrews	53	53 51	157
Bob Kirk, St Andrews	53	55 51	159
J.O.F. Morris, St Andrews	50	56 55	161
Bob Martin, St Andrews	57	53 55	165
*John Ball, Hoylake	53	57 55	165
Willie Park, Musselburgh	53	56 57	166
William Cosgrove, Musselburgh	53	56 55	166

1879 ST ANDREWS

Jamie Anderson, St Andrews	84 85	169
James Allan, Westward Ho!	88 84	172
Andrew Kirkaldy, St Andrews	86 86	172
George Paxton, Musselburgh		174
Tom Kidd, St Andrews		175
Bob Ferguson, Musselburgh		176

1880 MUSSELBURGH

Bob Ferguson, Musselburgh	81 81	162
Peter Paxton, Musselburgh	81 86	167
Ned Cosgrove, Musselburgh	82 86	168
George Paxton, Musselburgh	85 84	169
Bob Pringle, Musselburgh	90 79	169
David Brown, Musselburgh	86 83	169

1881 PRESTWICK

Bob Ferguson, Musselburgh	53	60 57	170
Jamie Anderson, St Andrews	57	60 56	173
Ned Cosgrove, Musselburgh	61	59 57	177
Bob Martin, St Andrews	57	62 59	178
Tom Morris Sr, St Andrews	58	65 58	181
Willie Campbell, Musselburgh	60	56 65	181
Willie Park Jr, Musselburgh	66	57 58	181

1882 ST ANDREWS

Bob Ferguson, Musselburgh	83 88	171
Willie Fernie, Dumfries	88 86	174
Jamie Anderson, St Andrews	87 88	175
John Kirkaldy, St Andrews	86 89	175
Bob Martin, St Andrews	89 86	175
*Fitz Boothby, St Andrews	86 89	175

1883 MUSSELBURGH

Willie Fernie, Dumfries	75 84	159
Bob Ferguson, Musselburgh	78 80	159
(Fernie won play-off 158 to 159)		
Willie Brown, Musselburgh	83 77	160
Bob Pringle, Musselburgh	79 82	161
Willie Campbell, Musselburgh	80 83	163
George Paxton, Musselburgh	80 83	163

1884 PRESTWICK

Jack Simpson, Carnoustie	78 82	160
David Rollan, Elie	81 83	164
Willie Fernie, Felixstowe	80 84	164
Willie Campbell, Musselburgh	84 85	169
Willie Park Jr, Musselburgh	86 83	169

1885 ST ANDREWS

Bob Martin, St Andrews	84 87	171
Archie Simpson, Carnoustie	83 89	172
David Ayton, St Andrews	89 84	173
Willie Fernie, Felixstowe	89 85	174
Willie Park Jr, Musselburgh	86 88	174
Bob Simpson, Carnoustie	85 89	174

1886 MUSSELBURGH

David Brown, Musselburgh	79 78	157
Willie Campbell, Musselburgh	78 81	159
Ben Campbell, Musselburgh	79 81	160
Archie Simpson, Carnoustie	82 79	161
Willie Park Jr, Musselburgh	84 77	161
Thomas Gossett, Musselburgh	82 79	161
Bob Ferguson, Musselburgh	82 79	161

1887 PRESTWICK

Willie Park Jr, Musselburgh	82 79	161
Bob Martin, St Andrews	81 81	162
Willie Campbell, Prestwick	77 87	164
*Johnny Laidlay, Honourable Company	86 80	166
Ben Sayers, North Berwick	83 85	168
Archie Simpson, Carnoustie	81 87	168

1888 ST ANDREWS

Jack Burns, Warwick	86 85	171
David Anderson Jr, St Andrews	86 86	172
Ben Sayers, North Berwick	85 87	172
Willie Campbell, Prestwick	84 90	174
*Leslie Balfour, Edinburgh	86 89	175

1889 MUSSELBURGH

Willie Park Jr, Musselburgh	39	39	39	38	155
Andrew Kirkaldy, St Andrews	39	38	39	39	155
(Park won play-off 158 to 163)					
Ben Sayes, North Berwick	39	40	41	39	159
*Johnny Laidlay, Honourable Company	42	39	40	41	162
David Brown, Musselburgh	43	39	41	39	162

1890 PRESTWICK

*John Ball, Royal Liverpool			82	82	164
Willie Fernie, Troon			85	82	167
Archie Simpson, Carnoustie			85	82	167
Willie Park Jr, Musselburgh			90	80	170
Andrew Kirkaldy, St Andrews			81	89	170

1891 ST ANDREWS

Hugh Kirkaldy, St Andrews			83	83	166
Willie Fernie, Troon			84	84	168
Andrew Kirkaldy, St Andrews			84	84	168
S. Mure Fergusson, Royal and Ancient			86	84	170
W.D. More, Chester			84	87	171
Willie Park Jr, Musselburgh			88	85	173

(From 1892 the competition was extended to 72 holes)

1892 MUIRFIELD

*Harold Hilton, Royal Liverpool	78	81	72	74	305
*John Ball Jr, Royal Liverpool	75	80	74	79	308
James Kirkaldy, St Andrews	77	83	73	75	308
Sandy Herd, Huddersfield	77	78	77	76	308
J. Kay, Seaton Carew	82	78	74	78	312
Ben Sayers, North Berwick	80	76	81	75	312

1893 PRESTWICK

Willie Auchterlonie, St Andrews	78	81	81	82	322
*Johnny Laidlay, Honourable Company	80	83	80	81	324
Sandy Herd, Huddersfield	82	81	78	84	325
Hugh Kirkaldy, St Andrews	83	79	82	82	326
Andrew Kirkaldy, St Andrews	85	82	82	77	326

1894 SANDWICH

J.H. Taylor, Winchester	84	80	81	81	326
Douglas Rolland, Limpsfield	86	79	84	82	331
Andrew Kirkaldy, St Andrews	86	79	83	84	332
A. Toogood, Eltham	84	85	82	82	333
Willie Fernie, Troon	84	84	86	80	334
Harry Vardon, Bury St Edmunds	86	86	82	80	334
Ben Sayers, North Berwick	85	81	84	84	334

1895 ST ANDREWS

J.H. Taylor, Winchester	86	78	80	78	322
Sandy Herd, Huddersfield	82	77	82	85	326
Andrew Kirkaldy, St Andrews	81	83	84	84	332
G. Pulford, Hoylake	84	81	83	87	335
Archie Simpson, Aberdeen	88	85	78	85	336

1896 MUIRFIELD

Harry Vardon, Ganton	83	78	78	77	316
J.H. Taylor, Winchester	77	78	81	80	316
(Vardon won play-off 157 to 161)					
*Freddie G. Tait, Black Watch	83	75	84	77	319
Willie Fernie, Troon	78	79	82	80	319
Sandy Herd, Huddersfield	72	84	79	85	320
James Braid, Romford	83	81	79	80	323

1897 HOYLAKE

*Harold H. Hilton, Royal Liverpool	80	75	84	75	314
James Braid, Romford	80	74	82	79	315
*Freddie G. Tait, Black Watch	79	79	80	79	317
G. Pulford, Hoylake	80	79	79	79	317
Sandy Herd, Huddersfield	78	81	79	80	318
Harry Vardon, Ganton	84	80	80	76	320

1898 PRESTWICK

Harry Vardon, Ganton	79	75	77	76	307
Willie Park, Musselburgh	76	75	78	79	308
*Harold H. Hilton, Royal Liverpool	76	81	77	75	309
J.H. Taylor, Winchester	78	78	77	79	312
*Freddie G. Tait, Black Watch	81	77	75	82	315

1899 SANDWICH

Harry Vardon, Ganton	76	76	81	77	310
Jack White, Seaford	79	79	82	75	315
Andrew Kirkaldy, St Andrews	81	79	82	77	319
J.H. Taylor, Mid-Surrey	77	76	83	84	320
James Braid, Romford	78	78	83	84	322
Willie Fernie, Troon	79	83	82	78	322

1900 ST ANDREWS

J.H. Taylor, Mid-Surrey	79	77	78	75	309
Harry Vardon, Ganton	79	81	80	78	317
James Braid, Romford	82	81	80	79	322
Jack White, Seaford	80	81	82	80	323
Willie Auchterlonie, St Andrews	81	85	80	80	326
Willie Park Jr, Musselburgh	80	83	81	84	328

1901 MUIRFIELD

James Braid, Romford	79	76	74	80	309
Harry Vardon, Ganton	77	78	79	78	312
J.H. Taylor, Mid-Surrey	79	83	74	77	313
*Harold H. Hilton, Royal Liverpool	89	80	75	76	320
Sandy Herd, Huddersfield	87	81	81	76	325
Jack White, Seaford	82	82	80	82	326

1902 HOYLAKE

Sandy Herd, Huddersfield	77	76	73	81	307
Harry Vardon, South Herts	72	77	80	79	308
James Braid, Walton Heath	78	76	80	74	308
R. Maxwell, Honourable Company	79	77	79	74	309
Tom Vardon, Ilkley	80	76	78	79	313
J.H. Taylor, Mid-Surrey	81	76	77	80	314
D. Kinnell, Leven	78	80	79	77	314
*Harold H. Hilton, Royal Liverpool	79	76	81	78	314

1903 PRESTWICK

Harry Vardon, South Herts	73	77	72	78	300
Tom Vardon, Ilkley	76	81	75	74	306
Jack White, Sunningdale	77	78	74	79	308
Sandy Herd, Huddersfield	73	83	76	77	309
James Braid, Walton Heath	77	79	79	75	310

1904 SANDWICH

Jack White, Sunningdale	80	75	72	69	296
James Braid, Walton Heath	77	80	69	71	297
J.H. Taylor, Mid-Surrey	77	78	74	68	297
Tom Vardon, Ilkley	77	77	75	72	301
Harry Vardon, South Herts	76	73	79	74	302

1905 ST ANDREWS

James Braid, Walton Heath	81	78	78	81	318
J.H. Taylor, Mid-Surrey	80	85	78	80	323
R. Jones, Wimbledon Park	81	77	87	78	323
J. Kinnell, Purley Downs	82	79	82	81	324
Arnaud Massy, La Boulie	81	80	82	82	325
E. Gray, Littlehampton	82	81	84	78	325

1906 MUIRFIELD

James Braid, Walton Heath	77	76	74	73	300
J.H. Taylor, Mid-Surrey	77	72	75	80	304
Harry Vardon, South Herts	77	73	77	78	305
*J. Graham Jr, Royal Liverpool	71	79	78	78	306
R. Jones, Wimbledon Park	74	78	73	83	308
Arnaud Massy, La Boulie	76	80	76	78	310

1907 HOYLAKE

Arnaud Massy, La Boulie	76	81	78	77	312
J.H. Taylor, Mid-Surrey	79	79	76	80	314
Tom Vardon, Sandwich	81	81	80	75	317
G. Pulford, Hoylake	81	78	80	78	317
Ted Ray, Ganton	83	80	79	76	318
James Braid, Walton Heath	82	85	75	76	318

1908 PRESTWICK

James Braid, Walton Heath	70	72	77	72	291
Tom Ball, West Lancashire	76	73	76	74	299
Ted Ray, Ganton	79	71	75	76	301
Sandy Herd, Huddersfield	74	74	79	75	302
Harry Vardon, South Herts	79	78	74	75	306
D. Kinnell, Prestwick St Nicholas	75	73	80	78	306

1909 DEAL

J.H. Taylor, Mid-Surrey	74	73	74	74	295
James Braid, Walton Heath	79	73	73	74	299
Tom Ball, West Lancashire	74	75	76	76	301
C. Johns, Southdown	72	76	79	75	302
T.G. Renouf, Manchester	76	78	76	73	303
Ted Ray, Ganton	77	76	76	75	304

1910 ST ANDREWS

James Braid, Walton Heath	76	73	74	76	299
Sandy Herd, Huddersfield	78	74	75	76	303
George Duncan, Hanger Hill	73	77	71	83	304
Laurie Ayton, Bishops Stortford	78	76	75	77	306
Ted Ray, Ganton	76	77	74	81	308
W. Smith, Mexico	77	71	80	80	308
J. Robson, West Surrey	75	80	77	76	308

1911 SANDWICH

Harry Vardon, South Herts	74	74	75	80	303
Arnaud Massy, St Jean de Luz	75	78	74	76	303
(Play-off; Massy conceded at the 35th hole)					

*Harold Hilton, Royal Liverpool	76	74	78	76	304
Sandy Herd, Coombe Hill	77	73	76	78	304
Ted Ray, Ganton	76	72	79	78	305
James Braid, Walton Heath	78	75	74	78	305
J.H. Taylor, Mid-Surrey	72	76	78	79	305

1912 MUIRFIELD

Ted Ray, Oxhey	71	73	76	75	295
Harry Vardon, South Herts	75	72	81	71	299
James Braid, Walton Heath	77	71	77	78	303
George Duncan, Hanger Hill	72	77	78	78	305
Laurie Ayton, Bishops Stortford	74	80	75	79	308

1913 HOYLAKE

J.H. Taylor, Mid-Surrey	73	75	77	79	304
Ted Ray, Oxhey	73	74	81	84	312
Harry Vardon, South Herts	79	75	79	80	313
M. Moran, Dollymount	76	74	89	74	313
Johnny J. McDermott, USA	75	80	77	83	315
T.G. Renouf, Manchester	75	78	84	78	315

1914 PRESTWICK

Harry Vardon, South Herts	73	77	78	78	306
J.H. Taylor, Mid-Surrey	74	78	74	83	309
H.B. Simpson, St Annes Old	77	80	78	75	310
Abe Mitchell, Sonning	76	78	79	79	312
Tom Williamson, Notts	75	79	79	79	312

1920 DEAL

George Duncan, Hanger Hill	80	80	71	72	303
Sandy Herd, Coombe Hill	72	81	77	75	305
Ted Ray, Oxhey	72	83	78	73	306
Abe Mitchell, North Foreland	74	73	84	76	307
Len Holland, Northampton	80	78	71	79	308
Jim Barnes, USA	79	74	77	79	309

1921 ST ANDREWS

Jock Hutchison, USA	72	75	79	70	296
*Roger Wethered, Royal and Ancient	78	75	72	71	296
(Hutchison won play-off 150 to 159)					
T. Kerrigan, USA	74	80	72	72	298
Arthur G. Havers, West Lancs	76	74	77	72	299
George Duncan, Hanger Hill	74	75	78	74	301

1922 SANDWICH

Walter Hagen, USA	76	73	79	72	300
George Duncan, Hangar Hill	76	75	81	69	301
Jim Barnes, USA	75	76	77	73	301
Jock Hutchison, USA	79	74	73	76	302
Charles Whitcombe, Dorchester	77	79	72	75	303
J.H. Taylor, Mid-Surrey	73	78	76	77	304

1923 TROON

Arthur G. Havers, Coombe Hill	73	73	73	76	295
Walter Hagen, USA	76	71	74	75	296
Macdonald Smith, USA	80	73	69	75	297
Joe Kirkwood, Australia	72	79	69	78	298
Tom Fernie, Turnberry	73	78	74	75	300

1924 HOYLAKE

Walter Hagen, USA	77	73	74	77	301
Ernest Whitcombe, Came Down	77	70	77	78	302
Macdonald Smith, USA	76	74	77	77	304
F. Ball, Langley Park	78	75	74	77	304
J.H. Taylor, Mid-Surrey	75	74	79	79	307

1925 PRESTWICK

Jim Barnes, USA	70	77	79	74	300
Archie Compston, North Manchester	76	75	75	75	301
Ted Ray, Oxhey	77	76	75	73	301
Macdonald Smith, USA	76	69	76	82	303
Abe Mitchell, Unattached	77	76	75	77	305

1926 ROYAL LYTHAM

*Robert T. Jones Jr, USA	72	72	73	74	291
Al Watrous, USA	71	75	69	78	293
Walter Hagen, USA	68	77	74	76	295
George von Elm, USA	75	72	76	72	295
Abe Mitchell, Unattached	78	78	72	71	299
T. Barber, Cavendish	77	73	78	71	299

1927 ST ANDREWS

*Robert T. Jones Jr, USA	68	72	73	72	285
Aubrey Boomer, St Cloud, Paris	76	70	73	72	291
Fred Robson, Cooden Beach	76	72	69	74	291
Joe Kirkwood, Australia	72	72	75	74	293
Ernest Whitcombe, Bournemouth	74	73	73	73	293

1928 SANDWICH

Walter Hagen, USA	75	73	72	72	292
Gene Sarazen, USA	72	76	73	73	294
Archie Compston, Unattached	75	74	73	73	295
Percy Alliss, Berlin	75	76	75	72	298
Fred Robson, Cooden Beach	79	73	73	73	298
Jose Jurado, Argentina	74	71	76	80	301
Aubrey Boomer, St Cloud, Paris	79	73	77	72	301
Jim Barnes, USA	81	73	76	71	301

1929 MUIRFIELD

Walter Hagen, USA	75	67	75	75	292
John Farrell, USA	72	75	76	75	298
Leo Diegel, USA	71	69	82	77	299
Abe Mitchell, St Albans	72	72	78	78	300
Percy Alliss, Berlin	69	76	76	79	300

1930 HOYLAKE

*Robert T. Jones Jr, USA	70	72	74	75	291
Leo Diegel, USA	74	73	71	75	293
Macdonald Smith, USA	70	77	75	71	293
Fred Robson, Cooden Beach	71	72	78	75	296
Horton Smith, USA	72	73	78	73	296
Archie Compston, Coombe Hill	74	73	68	82	297
Jim Barnes, USA	71	77	72	77	297

1931 CARNOUSTIE

Tommy Armour, USA	73	75	77	71	296
Jose Jurado, Argentina	76	71	73	77	297
Percy Alliss, Berlin	74	78	73	73	298
Gene Sarazen, USA	74	76	75	73	298
Macdonald Smith, USA	75	77	71	76	299
John Farrell, USA	72	77	75	75	299

1932 PRINCE'S

Gene Sarazen, USA	70	69	70	74	283
Macdonald Smith, USA	71	76	71	70	288
Arthur G. Havers, Sandy Lodge	74	71	68	76	289
Charles Whitcombe, Crews Hill	71	73	73	75	292
Percy Alliss, Beaconsfield	71	71	78	72	292
Alf Padgham, Royal Ashdown Forest	76	72	74	70	292

1933 ST ANDREWS

Densmore Shute, USA	73	73	73	73	292
Craig Wood, USA	77	72	68	75	292
(Shute won play-off 149 to 154)					
Sid Easterbrook, Knowle	73	72	71	77	293
Gene Sarazen, USA	72	73	73	75	293
Leo Diegel, USA	75	70	71	77	293

1934 SANDWICH

Henry Cotton, Waterloo, Belgium	67	65	72	79	283
Sid Brews, South Africa	76	71	70	71	288
Alf Padgham, Sundridge Park	71	70	75	74	290
Macdonald Smith, USA	77	71	72	72	292
Joe Kirkwood, USA	74	69	71	78	292
Marcel Dallemagne, France	71	73	71	77	292

1935 MUIRFIELD

Alf Perry, Leatherhead	69	75	67	72	283
Alf Padgham, Sundridge Park	70	72	74	71	287
Charles Whitcombe, Crews Hill	71	68	73	76	288
Bert Gadd, Brand Hall	72	75	71	71	289
Lawson Little, USA	75	71	74	69	289

1936 HOYLAKE

Alf Padgham, Sundridge Park	73	72	71	71	287
Jimmy Adams, Romford	71	73	71	73	288
Henry Cotton, Waterloo, Belgium	73	72	70	74	289
Marcel Dallemagne, France	73	72	75	69	289
Percy Alliss, Leeds Municipal	74	72	74	71	291
T. Green, Burnham Beeches	74	72	70	75	291
Gene Sarazen, USA	73	75	70	73	291

1937 CARNOUSTIE

Henry Cotton, Ashridge	74	72	73	71	290
Reg Whitcombe, Parkstone	72	70	74	76	292
Charles Lacey, USA	76	75	70	72	293
Charles Whitcombe, Crews Hill	73	71	74	76	294
Bryon Nelson, USA	75	76	71	74	296

1938 SANDWICH

Reg Whitcombe, Parkstone	71	71	75	78	295
Jimmy Adams, Royal Liverpool	70	71	78	78	297
Henry Cotton, Ashridge	74	73	77	74	298
Alf Padgham, Sundridge Park	74	72	75	82	303
Jack Busson, Pannal	71	69	83	80	303
Richard Burton, Sale	71	69	78	85	303
Allan Dailey, Wanstead	73	72	80	78	303

1939 ST ANDREWS

Richard Burton, Sale	70	72	77	71	290
Johnny Bulla, USA	77	71	71	73	292
Johnny Fallon, Huddersfield	71	73	71	79	294
Bill Shankland, Temple Newsam	72	73	72	77	294
Alf Perry, Leatherhead	71	74	73	76	294
Reg Whitcombe, Parkstone	71	75	74	74	294
Sam King, Knole Park	74	72	75	73	294

1946 ST ANDREWS

Sam Snead, USA	71	70	74	75	290
Bobby Locke, South Africa	69	74	75	76	294
Johnny Bulla, USA	71	72	72	79	294
Charlie Ward, Little Aston	73	73	73	76	295
Henry Cotton, Royal Mid-Surrey	70	70	76	79	295
Dai Rees, Hindhead	75	67	73	80	295
Norman von Nida, Australia	70	76	74	75	295

1947 HOYLAKE

Fred Daly, Balmoral, Belfast	73	70	78	72	293
Reg Horne, Hendon	77	74	72	71	294
*Frank Stranahan, USA	71	79	72	72	294
Bill Shankland, Temple Newsam	76	74	75	70	295
Richard Burton, Coombe Hill	77	71	77	71	296
Charlie Ward, Little Aston	76	73	76	72	297
Sam King, Wildernesse	75	72	77	73	297
Arthur Lees, Dore and Totley	75	74	72	76	297
Johnny Bulla, USA	80	72	74	71	297
Henry Cotton, Royal Mid-Surrey	69	78	74	76	297
Norman von Nida, Australia	74	76	71	76	297

1948 MUIRFIELD

Henry Cotton, Royal Mid-Surrey	71	66	75	72	284
Fred Daly, Balmoral, Belfast	72	71	73	73	289
Norman von Nida, Australia	71	72	76	71	290
Roberto de Vicenzo, Argentina	70	73	72	75	290
Jack Hargreaves, Sutton Coldfield	76	68	73	73	290
Charlie Ward, Little Aston	69	72	75	74	290

1949 SANDWICH

Bobby Locke, South Africa	69	76	68	70	283
Harry Bradshaw, Kilcroney, Eire	68	77	68	70	283
(Locke won play-off 135 to 147)					
Roberto de Vicenzo, Argentina	68	75	73	69	285
Sam King, Knole Park	71	69	74	72	286
Charlie Ward, Little Aston	73	71	70	72	286
Arthur Lees, Dore and Totley	74	70	72	71	287
Max Faulkner, Royal Mid-Surrey	71	71	71	74	287

1950 TROON

Bobby Locke, South Africa	69	72	70	68	279
Roberto de Vicenzo, Argentina	72	71	68	70	281
Fred Daly, Balmoral, Belfast	75	72	69	66	282
Dai Rees, South Herts	71	68	72	71	282
E. Moore, South Africa	74	68	73	68	283
Max Faulkner, Royal Mid-Surrey	73	70	70	71	283

1951 ROYAL PORTRUSH

Max Faulkner, Unattached	71	70	70	74	285
Tony Cerda, Argentina	74	72	71	70	287
Charlie Ward, Little Aston	75	73	74	68	290
Fred Daly, Balmoral, Belfast	74	70	75	73	292
Jimmy Adams, Wentworth	68	77	75	72	292
Bobby Locke, South Africa	71	74	74	74	293
Bill Shankland, Temple Newsam	73	76	72	72	293
Norman Sutton, Leigh	73	70	74	76	293
Harry Weetman, Croham Hurst	73	71	75	74	293
Peter Thomson, Australia	70	75	73	75	293

1952 ROYAL LYTHAM

Bobby Locke, South Africa	69	71	74	73	287
Peter Thomson, Australia	68	73	77	70	288
Fred Daly, Balmoral, Belfast	67	69	77	76	289
Henry Cotton, Royal Mid-Surrey	75	74	74	71	294
Tony Cerda, Argentina	73	73	76	73	295
Sam King, Knole Park	71	74	74	76	295

1953 CARNOUSTIE

Ben Hogan, USA	73	71	70	68	282
*Frank Stranahan, USA	70	74	73	69	286
Dai Rees, South Herts	72	70	73	71	286
Peter Thomson, Australia	72	72	71	71	286
Tony Cerda, Argentina	75	71	69	71	286
Roberto de Vicenzo, Argentina	72	71	71	73	287

1954 ROYAL BIRKDALE

Peter Thomson, Australia	72	71	69	71	283
Sid Scott, Carlisle City	76	67	69	72	284
Dai Rees, South Herts	72	71	69	72	284
Bobby Locke, South Africa	74	71	69	70	284
Jimmy Adams, Royal Mid-Surrey	73	75	69	69	286
Tony Cerda, Argentina	71	71	73	71	286
J. Turnesa, USA	72	72	71	71	286

1955 ST ANDREWS

Peter Thomson, Australia	71	68	70	72	281
Johnny Fallon, Huddersfield	73	67	73	70	283
Frank Jowle, Edgbaston	70	71	69	74	284
Bobby Locke, South Africa	74	69	70	72	285
Tony Cerda, Argentina	73	71	71	71	286
Ken Bousfield, Coombe Hill	71	75	70	70	286
Harry Weetman, Croham Hurst	71	71	70	74	286
Bernard Hunt, Hartsbourne	70	71	74	71	286
Flory van Donck, Belgium	71	72	71	72	286

1956 HOYLAKE

Peter Thomson, Australia	70	70	72	74	286
Flory van Donck, Belgium	71	74	70	74	289
Roberto de Vicenzo, Argentina	71	70	79	70	290
Gary Player, South Africa	71	76	73	71	291
John Panton, Glenbervie	74	76	72	70	292
Henry Cotton, Temple	72	76	71	74	293
E. Bertolino, Argentina	69	72	76	76	293

1957 ST ANDREWS

Bobby Locke, South Africa	69	72	68	70	279
Peter Thomson, Australia	73	69	70	70	282
Eric Brown, Buchanan Castle	67	72	73	71	283
Angel Miguel, Spain	72	72	69	72	285
David Thomas, Sudbury	72	74	70	70	286
Tom Haliburton, Wentworth	72	73	68	73	286
*Dick Smith, Prestwick	71	72	72	71	286
Flory van Donck, Belgium	72	68	74	72	286

1958 ROYAL LYTHAM

Peter Thomson, Australia	66	72	67	73	278
David Thomas, Sudbury	70	68	69	71	278
(Thomson won play-off 139 to 143)					
Eric Brown, Buchanan Castle	73	70	65	71	279
Christy O'Connor, Killarney	67	68	73	71	279
Flory van Donck, Belgium	70	70	67	74	281
Leopoldo Ruiz, Argentina	71	65	72	73	281

1959 MUIRFIELD

Gary Player, South Africa	75	71	70	68	284
Flory van Donck, Belgium	70	70	73	73	286
Fred Bullock, Prestwick	68	70	74	74	286
St Ninians					
Sid Scott, Roehampton	73	70	73	71	287
Christy O'Connor, Royal Dublin	73	74	72	69	288
*Reid Jack, Dullatur	71	75	68	74	288
Sam King, Knole Park	70	74	68	76	288
John Panton, Glenbervie	72	72	71	73	288

1960 ST ANDREWS

Kel Nagle, Australia	69	67	71	71	278
Arnold Palmer, USA	70	71	70	68	279
Bernard Hunt, Hartsbourne	72	73	71	66	282
Harold Henning, South Africa	72	72	69	69	282
Roberto de Vicenzo, Argentina	67	67	75	73	282

1961 ROYAL BIRKDALE

Arnold Palmer, USA	70	73	69	72	284
Dai Rees, South Herts	68	74	71	72	285
Christy O'Connor, Royal Dublin	71	77	67	73	288
Neil Coles, Coombe Hill	70	77	69	72	288
Eric Brown, Unattached	73	76	70	70	289
Kel Nagle, Australia	68	75	75	71	289

1962 TROON

Arnold Palmer, USA	71	69	67	69	276
Kel Nagle, Australia	71	71	70	70	282
Brian Huggett, Romford	75	71	74	69	289
Phil Rodgers, USA	75	70	72	72	289
Bob Charles, NZ	75	70	70	75	290
Sam Snead, USA	76	73	72	71	292
Peter Thomson, Australia	70	77	75	70	292

1963 ROYAL LYTHAM

Bob Charles, NZ	68	72	66	71	277
Phil Rodgers, USA	67	68	73	69	277
(Charles won play-off 140 to 148)					
Jack Nicklaus, USA	71	67	70	70	278
Kel Nagle, Australia	69	70	73	71	283
Peter Thomson, Australia	67	69	71	78	285

1964 ST ANDREWS

Tony Lema, USA	73	68	68	70	279
Jack Nicklaus, USA	76	74	66	68	284
Roberto de Vicenzo, Argentina	76	72	70	67	285
Bernard Hunt, Hartsbourne	73	74	70	70	287
Bruce Devlin, Australia	72	72	73	73	290

1965 ROYAL BIRKDALE

Peter Thomson, Australia	74	68	72	71	285
Christy O'Connor, Royal Dublin	69	73	74	71	287
Brian Huggett, Romford	73	68	76	70	287
Roberto de Vicenzo, Argentina	74	69	73	72	288
Kel Nagle, Australia	74	70	73	72	289
Tony Lema, USA	68	72	75	74	289
Bernard Hunt, Hartsbourne	74	74	70	71	289

1966 MUIRFIELD

Jack Nicklaus, USA	70	67	75	70	282
David Thomas, Dunham Forest	72	73	69	69	283
Doug Sanders, USA	71	70	72	70	283
Gary Player, South Africa	72	74	71	69	286
Bruce Devlin, Australia	73	69	74	70	286
Kel Nagle, Australia	72	68	76	70	286
Phil Rodgers, USA	74	66	70	76	286

1967 HOYLAKE

Roberto de Vicenzo, Argentina	70	71	67	70	278
Jack Nicklaus, USA	71	69	71	69	280
Clive Clark, Sunningdale	70	73	69	72	284
Gary Player, South Africa	72	71	67	74	284
Tony Jacklin, Potters Bar	73	69	73	70	285

1968 CARNOUSTIE

Gary Player, South Africa	74	71	71	73	289
Jack Nicklaus, USA	76	69	73	73	291
Bob Charles, NZ	72	72	71	76	291
Billy Casper, USA	72	68	74	78	292
Maurice Bembridge, Little Aston	71	75	73	74	293

1969 ROYAL LYTHAM

Tony Jacklin, Potters Bar	68	70	70	72	280
Bob Charles, NZ	66	69	75	72	282
Peter Thomson, Australia	71	70	70	72	283
Roberto de Vicenzo, Argentina	72	73	66	72	283
Christy O'Connor, Royal Dublin	71	65	74	74	284
Jack Nicklaus, USA	75	70	68	72	285
Davis Love Jr, USA	70	73	71	71	285

1970 ST ANDREWS

Jack Nicklaus, USA	68	69	73	73	283
Doug Sanders, USA	68	71	71	73	283
(Nicklaus won play-off 72 to 73)					
Harold Henning, South Africa	67	72	73	73	285
Lee Trevino, USA	68	68	72	77	285
Tony Jacklin, Potters Bar	67	70	73	76	286

1971 ROYAL BIRKDALE

Lee Trevino, USA	69	70	69	70	278
Lu Liang Huan, Taiwan	70	70	69	70	279
Tony Jacklin, Potters Bar	69	70	70	71	280
Craig de Foy, Coombe Hill	72	72	68	69	281
Jack Nicklaus, USA	71	71	72	69	283
Charles Coody, USA	74	71	70	68	283

1972 MUIRFIELD

Lee Trevino, USA	71	70	66	71	278
Jack Nicklaus, USA	70	72	71	66	279
Tony Jacklin, Potters Bar	69	72	67	72	280
Doug Sanders, USA	71	71	69	70	281
Brian Barnes, Fairway DR	71	72	69	71	283
Gary Player, South Africa	71	71	76	67	285

1973 TROON

Tom Weiskopf, USA	68	67	71	70	276
Neil Coles, Holiday Inns	71	72	70	66	279
Johnny Miller, USA	70	68	69	72	279
Jack Nicklaus, USA	69	70	76	65	280
Bert Yancey, USA	69	69	73	70	281

1974 ROYAL LYTHAM

Gary Player, South Africa	69	68	75	70	282
Peter Oosterhuis, Pacific Harbour	71	71	73	71	286
Jack Nicklaus, USA	74	72	70	71	287
Hubert Green, USA	71	74	72	71	288
Danny Edwards, USA	70	73	76	73	292
Lu Liang Huan, Taiwan	72	72	75	73	292

1975 CARNOUSTIE

Tom Watson, USA	71	67	69	72	279
Jack Newton, Australia	69	71	65	74	279
(Watson won play-off 71 to 72)					
Bobby Cole, South Africa	72	66	66	76	280
Jack Nicklaus, USA	69	71	68	72	280
Johnny Miller, USA	71	69	66	74	280

1976 ROYAL BIRKDALE

Johnny Miller, USA	72	68	73	66	279
Jack Nicklaus, USA	74	70	72	69	285
Severiano Ballesteros, Spain	69	69	73	74	285
Raymond Floyd, USA	76	67	73	70	286
Mark James, Burghley Park	76	72	74	66	288
Hubert Green, USA	72	70	78	68	288
Christy O'Connor Jr, Shannon	69	73	75	71	288
Tom Kite, USA	70	74	73	71	288
Tommy Horton, Royal Jersey	74	69	72	73	288

1977 TURNBERRY

Tom Watson, USA	68	70	65	65	268
Jack Nicklaus, USA	68	70	65	66	269
Hubert Green, USA	72	66	74	67	279
Lee Trevino, USA	68	70	72	70	280
Ben Crenshaw, USA	71	69	66	75	281
George Burns, USA	70	70	72	69	281

1978 ST ANDREWS

Jack Nicklaus, USA	71	72	69	69	281
Simon Owen, NZ	70	75	67	71	283
Ben Crenshaw, USA	70	69	73	71	283
Raymond Floyd, USA	69	75	71	68	283
Tom Kite, USA	72	69	72	70	283

1979 ROYAL LYTHAM

Severiano Ballesteros, Spain	73	65	75	70	283
Jack Nicklaus, USA	72	69	73	72	286
Ben Crenshaw, USA	72	71	72	71	286
Mark James, Burghley Park	76	69	69	73	287
Rodger Davis, Australia	75	70	70	73	288

1980 MUIRFIELD

Tom Watson, USA	68	70	64	69	271
Lee Trevino, USA	68	67	71	69	275
Ben Crenshaw, USA	70	70	68	69	277
Jack Nicklaus, USA	73	67	71	69	280
Carl Mason, Unattached	72	69	70	69	280

1981 SANDWICH

Bill Rogers, USA	72	66	67	71	276
Bernhard Langer, Germany	73	67	70	70	280
Mark James, Otley	72	70	68	73	283
Raymond Floyd, USA	74	70	69	70	283
Sam Torrance, Caledonian Hotel	72	69	73	70	284

1982 TROON

Tom Watson, USA	69	71	74	70	284
Peter Oosterhuis, GB	74	67	74	70	285
Nick Price, South Africa	69	69	74	73	285
Nick Faldo, Glynwed Ltd	73	73	71	69	286
Des Smyth, EAL Tubes	70	69	74	73	286
Tom Purtzer, USA	76	66	75	69	286
Massy Kuramoto, Japan	71	73	71	71	286

1983 ROYAL BIRKDALE

Tom Watson, USA	67	68	70	70	275
Hale Irwin, USA	69	68	72	67	276
Andy Bean, USA	70	69	70	67	276
Graham Marsh, Australia	69	70	74	64	277
Lee Trevino, USA	69	66	73	70	278
Severiano Ballesteros, Spain	71	71	69	68	279
Harold Henning, South Africa	71	69	70	69	279

1984 ST ANDREWS

Severiano Ballesteros, Spain	69	68	70	69	276
Bernhard Langer, Germany	71	68	68	71	278
Tom Watson, USA	71	68	66	73	278
Fred Couples, USA	70	69	74	68	281
Lanny Wadkins, USA	70	69	73	69	281
Greg Norman, Australia	67	74	74	67	282
Nick Faldo, Glynwed Int.	69	68	76	69	282

1985 SANDWICH

Sandy Lyle, Scotland	68	71	73	70	282
Payne Stewart, USA	70	75	70	68	283
Jose Rivero, Spain	74	72	70	68	284
Christy O'Connor Jr, Ireland	64	76	72	72	284
Mark O'Meara, USA	70	72	70	72	284
David Graham, Australia	68	71	70	75	284
Bernhard Langer, Germany	72	69	68	75	284

1986 TURNBERRY

Greg Norman, Australia	74	63	74	69	280
Gordon J. Brand, England	71	68	75	71	285
Bernhard Langer, Germany	72	70	76	68	286
Ian Woosnam, Wales	70	74	70	72	286
Nick Faldo, England	71	70	76	70	287

1987 MUIRFIELD

Nick Faldo, England	68	69	71	71	279
Rodger Davis, Australia	64	73	74	69	280
Paul Azinger, USA	68	68	71	73	280
Ben Crenshaw, USA	73	68	72	68	281
Payne Stewart, USA	71	66	72	72	281

1988 ROYAL LYTHAM

Severiano Ballesteros, Spain	67	71	70	65	273
Nick Price, Zimbabwe	70	67	69	69	275
Nick Faldo, England	71	69	68	71	279
Fred Couples, USA	73	69	71	68	281
Gary Koch, USA	71	72	70	68	281

1989 ROYAL TROON

Mark Calcavecchia, USA	71	68	68	68	275
Greg Norman, Australia	69	70	72	64	275
Wayne Grady, Australia	68	67	69	71	275
(Calcavecchia won four-hole play-off)					
Tom Watson, USA	69	68	68	72	277
Jodie Mudd, USA	73	67	68	70	278

1990 ST ANDREWS

Nick Faldo, England	67	65	67	71	270
Mark McNulty, Zimbabwe	74	68	68	65	275
Payne Stewart, USA	68	68	68	71	275
Jodie Mudd, USA	72	66	72	66	276
Ian Woosnam, Wales	68	69	70	69	276

1991 ROYAL BIRKDALE

Ian Baker-Finch, Australia	71	71	64	66	272
Mike Harwood, Australia	68	70	69	67	274
Fred Couples, USA	72	69	70	64	275
Mark O'Meara, USA	71	68	67	69	275
Jodie Mudd, USA	72	70	72	63	277
Bob Tway, USA	75	66	70	66	277
Eamonn Darcy, Ireland	73	68	66	70	277

1992 MUIRFIELD

Nick Faldo, England	66	64	69	73	272
John Cook, USA	66	67	70	70	273
Jose Maria Olazabal, Spain	70	67	69	68	274
Steve Pate, USA	64	70	69	73	276
Andrew Magee, USA	67	72	70	70	279
Malcolm Mackenzie, England	71	67	70	71	279
Robert Karlsson, Sweden	70	68	70	71	279
Ian Woosnam, Wales	65	73	70	71	279
Gordon Brand Jr, Scotland	65	68	72	74	279
Donnie Hammond, USA	70	65	70	74	279
Ernie Els, South Africa	66	69	70	74	279

FINAL RESULTS

HOLE		1	2	3	4	5	6	7	8	9	10	11	12	13	14	15	16	17	18	
PAR		4	4	3	4	4	3	5	4	4	4	3	4	4	5	4	3	4	4	TOTAL
Greg Norman	Round 1	6	3	3	4	3	4	4	4	4	4	4	4	3	4	3	2	3	4	66
	Round 2	4	3	3	4	5	2	5	4	4	3	3	3	3	5	4	3	5	4	68
	Round 3	3	4	3	4	4	3	5	4	4	4	2	4	4	5	5	3	4	4	69
	Round 4	3	4	2	4	4	2	5	4	3	4	3	3	4	4	4	2	5	4	64-267
Nick Faldo	Round 1	4	4	3	4	3	2	4	4	4	4	3	5	4	5	4	3	5	4	69
	Round 2	3	4	3	4	3	2	4	4	4	4	3	4	3	4	4	3	4	3	63
	Round 3	4	3	3	5	4	3	5	4	4	4	3	4	4	5	4	3	4	4	70
	Round 4	4	3	3	5	4	2	5	4	4	4	2	4	4	4	4	3	4	4	67-269
Bernhard Langer	Round 1	4	3	3	4	4	3	4	4	4	4	3	4	4	4	4	4	3	4	67
	Round 2	3	4	3	4	4	3	4	3	4	4	2	4	4	4	4	3	4	5	66
	Round 3	4	3	3	4	4	4	4	6	4	4	3	4	4	5	4	2	4	4	70
	Round 4	3	4	3	5	3	3	4	4	4	4	4	3	3	7	3	2	4	4	67-270
Peter Senior	Round 1	4	3	3	4	3	3	5	3	3	4	4	4	3	5	4	3	4	4	66
	Round 2	4	4	2	5	4	3	4	4	4	4	3	3	4	5	5	3	5	4	69
	Round 3	4	4	3	5	4	3	3	4	4	4	3	4	5	5	4	3	4	4	70
	Round 4	5	4	3	4	4	3	4	4	4	3	3	4	4	4	3	2	4	5	67-272
Corey Pavin	Round 1	4	4	3	4	3	3	3	3	4	5	3	4	5	5	4	2	4	4	68
	Round 2	4	4	4	4	4	2	4	4	3	4	3	3	5	3	3	3	5	4	66
	Round 3	4	3	3	3	4	3	5	4	4	4	3	4	4	5	5	2	4	4	68
	Round 4	5	3	3	5	4	4	4	4	4	4	4	3	4	4	3	3	5	4	70-272
Paul Lawrie	Round 1	5	4	3	4	4	3	4	3	4	4	4	4	4	6	4	3	5	4	72
	Round 2	4	3	3	4	5	3	3	4	5	4	3	4	3	5	3	4	4	4	68
	Round 3	4	4	3	3	4	3	4	4	4	4	3	4	5	5	4	2	4	5	69
	Round 4	4	3	3	4	4	3	5	4	3	4	2	4	4	4	4	3	2	5	65-274
Ernie Els	Round 1	4	4	2	4	5	2	5	3	4	4	4	4	4	5	4	3	3	4	68
	Round 2	4	3	4	4	5	2	4	4	4	4	3	3	4	6	5	3	3	4	69
	Round 3	3	3	3	4	3	3	5	3	5	4	3	4	4	5	5	3	4	5	69
	Round 4	3	5	3	4	4	3	4	4	4	3	4	3	4	4	4	3	4	5	68-274
Nick Price	Round 1	4	3	4	5	4	3	4	4	4	4	3	3	4	4	4	2	5	4	68
	Round 2	4	4	3	4	4	3	4	4	4	4	4	4	4	5	4	4	4	4	70
	Round 3	3	3	3	4	4	3	4	4	4	5	3	3	3	5	4	4	4	4	67
	Round 4	4	3	3	4	3	3	5	5	3	5	4	5	4	4	4	3	3	4	69-274
Scott Simpson	Round 1	4	4	3	4	4	3	4	4	5	4	3	3	4	4	6	2	3	4	68
	Round 2	3	4	3	5	4	3	5	3	4	4	4	4	3	5	4	3	4	5	70
	Round 3	4	4	3	5	4	3	4	4	4	5	2	4	5	4	5	3	4	4	71
	Round 4	3	4	3	5	4	2	4	4	4	4	3	3	4	5	4	2	4	4	66-275
Fred Couples	Round 1	4	4	3	5	5	3	4	4	4	4	3	4	3	4	4	3	4	3	68
	Round 2	4	3	2	4	4	3	4	5	3	4	3	3	3	4	4	3	5	5	66
	Round 3	4	4	3	5	4	3	6	5	4	3	3	4	4	5	4	2	5	4	72
	Round 4	4	4	3	4	4	2	5	4	4	4	3	3	4	4	4	3	5	5	69-275
Wayne Grady	Round 1	5	4	4	5	4	3	5	4	5	4	2	5	5	5	3	3	4	4	74
	Round 2	4	4	3	4	4	2	4	4	4	4	3	3	4	5	4	4	4	4	68
	Round 3	3	3	3	4	4	3	3	3	4	3	3	4	4	5	4	3	4	4	64
	Round 4	4	4	3	5	5	3	3	5	4	4	3	4	3	5	4	2	4	4	69-275

Peter Coleman and Bernhard Langer

Tony Navarro and Greg Norman

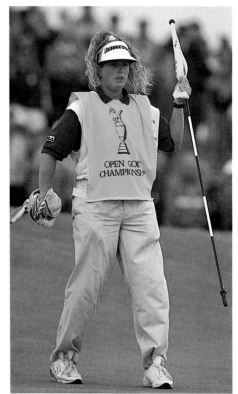

Fanny Sunesson (Nick Faldo)   Steve Williams (Raymond Floyd)   Greg Rita (John Daly)

Gary and Jack Nicklaus

Bruce Edwards (Tom Watson)

Jeff (Squeaky) Medlen (Nick Price)

Mike Hicks (Payne Stewart)

Joe LaCava and Fred Couples

THE ROYAL
ST. GEORGE'S
GOLF CLUB
SANDWICH

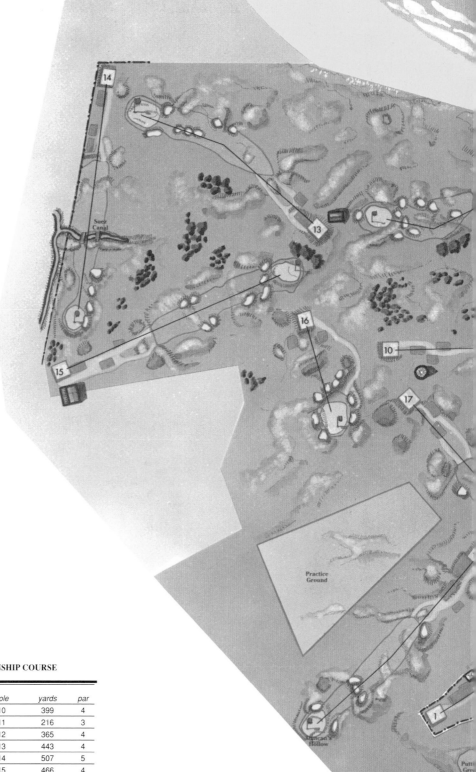

CARD OF THE CHAMPIONSHIP COURSE

hole	yards	par	hole	yards	par
1	441	4	10	399	4
2	376	4	11	216	3
3	210	3	12	365	4
4	468	4	13	443	4
5	421	4	14	507	5
6	155	3	15	466	4
7	530	5	16	163	3
8	418	4	17	425	4
9	389	4	18	468	4
OUT	3,408	35	IN	3,452	35
			OUT	3,408	35
			TOTAL	6,860	70